To Jim,
 with gratitude
 And much
 Admiration!

10.30.14

Iran's Strategic Penetration of
Latin America

Iran's Strategic Penetration of Latin America

Edited by Joseph M. Humire and Ilan Berman

Foreword by Marta Lucía Ramírez

LEXINGTON BOOKS
Lanham • Boulder • New York • London

Published by Lexington Books
An imprint of The Rowman & Littlefield Publishing Group, Inc.
4501 Forbes Boulevard, Suite 200, Lanham, Maryland 20706
www.rowman.com

16 Carlisle Street, London W1D 3BT, United Kingdom

British Library Cataloguing in Publication Information Available

Library of Congress Cataloging-in-Publication Data

Iran's strategic penetration of Latin America / edited by Ilan Berman, Joseph M. Humire.
p. cm.
Includes bibliographical references and index.
ISBN 978-0-7391-8266-6 (cloth : alk. paper) – ISBN 978-0-7391-8267-3 (ebook)
1. Latin America–Foreign relations–Iran. 2. Iran–Foreign relations–Latin America. 3. Iran–Foreign
relations–1979- I. Berman, Ilan, editor of compilation. II. Humire, Joseph M., 1979- editor of compilation.
F1416.I72I74 2014
327.8055–dc23
2014030856

Printed in the United States of America

For those continuing to fight for freedom and security in
Latin America and the Middle East.

Contents

Acknowledgments

A number of individuals inspired, supported and assisted in the creation of this book. They include Dr. Max Manwaring of the U.S. Army War College, whose teachings on asymmetric warfare inspired me to put my ideas and experience into this project. I would also like to acknowledge Ambassador Curtin Winsor, Anita Winsor, Alejandro Chafuen, Abby Moffat, and George Lengvari for their invaluable support, which made the research of this book possible.

Several dedicated professionals from the U.S. intelligence, defense and law enforcement community, particularly within U.S. Special Operations Command, deserve my gratitude for providing additional insights toward understanding threats in Latin America and the Middle East. So does one of the nation's top experts on Iran, my co-editor Ilan Berman, who has opened my eyes to the growing global network of the Islamic Republic. Several former interns of the Center for a Secure Free Society (SFS) also deserve my gratitude, namely Rachel Echeto and Renzo Falla, whose hard work helped realize this publication. Special thanks also go out to Fernando Menéndez, J.D. Gordon, Ignacio Ibáñez, Douglas Farah, Dardo Lopez-Dolz, Ricardo Neeb, and Roger Pardo-Maurer, who provided me with indispensable intellectual advice.

Lastly, of course, I cannot forget to extend a heartfelt thanks to my family and friends, particularly Angelica Herrera, Ross Armstrong, and Rudy Escobar for their encouragement; to my father, Luis Humire, for his support; to my uncle, John Hartranft, for his confidence; and my two brothers, Daniel and Bryan, who always force me to be more critical in my analysis. And especially to my lovely mother, Leticia Humire, who is the source of my strength. Special thanks also go out to Vision Americas, Fernando Menéndez, J.D. Gordon, Ignacio Ibáñez, Douglas Farah, Dardo Lopez-Dolz, Ricardo Neeb, and Roger Pardo-Maurer, who provided me with indispensable intellectual advice.

Joseph Humire
Washington, D.C.
July 2014

* * * * * *

Compilations like this one are, inevitably, labors of love for all those who embark upon them. They are also, more often than not, a team effort. This volume is no different; it simply would not have been possible without the assistance of experts, both in the United States and abroad, who lent their considerable intellects to the cause. Many of them cannot be mentioned, either because of sensitive government positions or as a result of delicate political circumstances, but all of them deserve my profound thanks.

Special thanks as well goes out to American Foreign Policy Council (AFPC) president Herman Pirchner, who was tireless in his support and encouragement of this project, as he has been on so many other occasions. I am also grateful to Jessica Sardella, Camilla Paez and the other interns at AFPC who helped in the research, editing, and formatting of this work.

Finally, I extend my heartfelt appreciation to my co-editor Joseph Humire, who is both a true expert on Latin America and a tireless travel companion. Over the years, his advice and insights have guided me in my exploration of the region, from Chile to Bolivia to Nicaragua and beyond.

Ilan Berman
Washington, D.C.
July 2014

Foreword

Many contemporary political analysts claim that history is currently at a "crossroads." Indeed, we are witnessing a rapid and profound transformation of the established world order. However, history tells us that when such political change is pushed by extremists, there are often devastating effects on the social, economic, and political fabric of modern society.

For over two decades, in my role as a political leader and policy maker in Colombia, I have worked to neutralize these radical forces in Latin America. But, as this book reveals all too clearly, we remain under threat. And among the most complex security challenges in the Western Hemisphere today is the intrusion of nontraditional foreign forces, such as the Islamic Republic of Iran.

Venezuela's outsized role in providing a gateway to Iran into the region, complete with arms deals, military transfers, and clandestine intelligence cooperation, are proof that times have indeed changed. The Bolivarian Republic's "axis of unity" with Iran embodies Latin America's growing distance from its traditional ally, the United States. And although the era of Hugo Chávez and his close friend Mahmoud Ahmadinejad has passed, many commercial, political, and military ties remain. The subsequent pages of this book cover many of these activities in detail, so I will not go into depth on the subject matter. I will, nonetheless, make a call for the United States to take this alliance seriously and act forcefully in the region. Countering the influence of non-traditional, extra-regional forces in Latin America requires U.S. engagement. This is not to distract from the many conflicts the United States is engaging in the Middle East or elsewhere, but rather to remind our northern neighbors of the kind of disengagement in Latin America that led to a nuclear standoff in 1962.

My concern does not come from simply Venezuela's role in this protracted, asymmetric struggle—but the growing proximity between many nations in Latin America and Iran and other controversial extra-regional actors. Unfortunately, Latin America is quietly drifting away from its once-emerging democratic institutions and adopting a dangerous "cult of personality," in which populist, authoritarian leaders consolidate power within national governments and define the course of their countries undemocratically. This trend is visible in Argentina, Brazil, Bolivia and Ecuador, and is deeply worrying for those of us who work to maintain a democratic tradition in Latin America aimed at growth, development, social welfare, and the guarantee of individual liberty.

These strong winds of populist change have shifted the political transformation of Latin America causing confrontations between several nations in the region, and could possibly lead to more internal and international conflict. The roots of this phenomenon are not only within the political realm, but are also driven by economic incentives that correspond to larger geopolitical agendas. Ecuador and Bolivia are especially worrying in this regard, because they may soon replace Venezuela as Iran's most important strategic partners in the region, subsequently adopting policy positions that do not favor the West. Even traditional U.S. allies such as Chile are shifting away from their long-standing political orientation in what amounts to a warning of things to come.

My own country, Colombia, can be counted as perhaps the strongest ally of the United States in the region. But it is also heading toward a drastic shift in its political direction—a change that could quite possibly lead to its socioeconomic decline. The Colombian government's ongoing peace talks with the Revolutionary Armed Forces of Colombia (FARC) have enabled radical factions within the country, which were traditionally excluded from politics, to gain influence over key policymaking positions. These factions do not favor increased commerce and dialogue with the United States, and will seek to replace U.S. influence in Colombia with that of other nations, such as Iran, if their political power continues to grow. In order for this not to happen, it is imperative that Latin America becomes a greater policy priority for the United States.

This bleak picture should not be interpreted as reason for hopelessness or despair. Rather, it should spur a call for increased attention, cooperation, and unity among the democratic countries of the Western Hemisphere. This is not a situation dissimilar to others we have faced and conquered in the past. In our personal lives, we have all had close friends that have helped us grow and become better persons. As time goes by, these friendships can become distant as we are drawn to others less beneficial to our wellbeing. Then we see our old friends again, catch up on lost times, and the past quickly becomes the present, as we remember what made us strong, what motivated us, and the bond that brought us together. Our shared history and collective memory reminds us that our past and our future are closely related because this bond is the base to renew and refuel even greater cooperation and friendship in the future. For the United States and other countries seeking to reengage our region, this is the key to our success.

This volume, of which I have had the honor of writing the foreword, can serve as a wakeup call for a renewed conversation. The book will explain new problems and describe difficult developments, but in the end should bring us together to begin to address these challenges. My thanks therefore go to Joseph Humire, Ilan Berman, and all the contributors to this book, for highlighting a growing—and as yet underappreciated—security challenge affecting the countries of the Americas, and by doing so starting a long overdue but sorely needed conversation between old friends.

Marta Lucía Ramírez
Former National Defense and Foreign Trade Minister of Colombia

Preface

Iran's Intrusion: An Overview

Joseph Humire

In May of 2012, intelligence and security services throughout Latin America were on high alert for a potential Iranian-sponsored terror attack in South America. This largely overlooked development followed a report by well-respected journalist Guido Olimpio of the Italian daily *Corriere della Sera* of a potential attack in Brazil or Colombia being organized by a terror network related to the Quds Force, the elite paramilitary unit of Iran's Revolutionary Guards, and the Lebanese terrorist group Hezbollah.[1] The threat was credible, because this same network had successfully carried out a bomb attack in New Delhi, India, as well as attempting a similar bombing in Bangkok, Thailand, earlier that year. And although the aforementioned plot did not materialize, the regional mobilization that ensued speaks volumes about how seriously authorities in Latin America took the threat—and how clear and present they believe the danger from Iran and Iranian-supported militants to truly be.

Recent years have seen growing attention being paid to the phenomenon of Iran's influence in Latin America. Yet most analysts and policymakers still focus too much attention on Iran's formal activities in the Americas, and its political motivations for engaging the region. However, as Olimpio's reporting underscores, there is much more happening beneath the surface. The purpose of this book is to examine those activities as a way of revealing what Iran does not want the world to know: that it views Latin America as a latent theater of operation, and that it is building its capacity and capability throughout the Americas.

Iran's strategic penetration of Latin America began in earnest shortly after the 1979 Iranian Revolution through clandestine networks that operated under the guise of cultural and commercial exchanges. At the turn of this century, the rise of Venezuelan strongman Hugo Chávez and his "Bolivarian revolution" spurred a dramatic expansion of Iran's diplomatic and economic presence in the region. This overt presence, in turn, has sparked debate throughout the Hemisphere regarding Iran's motives south of the U.S. border.

Skeptical observers point to the fact that most of Iran's promises to Latin American countries remain unfulfilled, and take that to mean that Iran's presence remains negligible.[2] Yet this analysis ignores the fact that most of Iran's regional activities are covert in nature. Understanding the complexity of Iran's influence in Latin America therefore requires a bottom-up approach that harnesses the local knowledge necessary to truly determine the extent and gravity of the threat.

This volume attempts to do so, and the various chapters contained herein are written by some of the region's foremost authorities on the subject. These experts have been examining Iran's intrusion into Latin America for years, and doing so from the ground level as former military and intelligence officers, congressmen, investigative journalists, academics, and scholars from Chile, Brazil, Ecuador, Venezuela, Bolivia, Argentina and the United States.

In the first chapter, co-editor Ilan Berman explains Iran's strategic objectives in Latin America, and how they relate to the regime's pursuit of a global strategic footprint and a nuclear capability. In the second and third chapters, American scholars Jon Perdue and Joel Hirst delve into the underlying motivations for Iran's presence in the Americas. Perdue provides a historical overview of the ideological kinship between Islamic radicalism and Latin American socialism, highlighting the shared militancy that binds the leftist Latin American leaders to the radical theocratic regime in Tehran. Hirst introduces us to the political power project that has been dominating regional politics for over a decade—the Bolivarian Alliance of the Americas, or ALBA—and explains the pragmatic benefits that a symbiotic relationship between ALBA and Iran can offer to those seeking a "new world order."

The nations of ALBA, particularly Venezuela and Cuba, are widely considered to be Iran's gateways into Latin America. Chapter four, however, introduces a potential backdoor further south through the Andes. Chilean academic Iván Witker provides a country-by-country analysis of how the Southern Cone region can complement Iran's already-extensive presence in Venezuela and Bolivia.

In the fifth chapter, we begin to transition from the strategic to the tactical. Award-winning Brazilian investigative journalist Leonardo Coutinho exposes the thriving clandestine network of Islamic extremists that exists today in Brazil—a network that Iran is using to gradually gain political favor there. In chapter six, Alex Pérez (a *nom de plume*), introduces us to a relatively unknown alternative currency system being developed in Ecuador, called the

SUCRE, and details how Iran has laid the groundwork to potentially use this system as the perfect sanctions busting tool should its current nuclear negotiations with the West fail.

While evading sanctions are a concern, a potentially more concerning effort is underway in Venezuela. Arguably the country that has provided the most benefits to Iran in Latin America, Venezuela has become the hub for Iran's military ambitions in the region. In chapter seven, Martin Rodil, a Venezuelan counter-threat finance expert, provides damning details of how Iran has established a military industrial footprint in a country situated only two-and-a-half hours from Florida. Supplementing this analysis, Bolivian congressman Adrián Oliva explains, in chapter eight, how Iran has gradually increased its military presence in Bolivia, including its role in the construction of a new regional defense school near the commercial city of Santa Cruz.

Possibly the most controversial of Iran's activities in Latin America to date has been its attempt to rewrite history by initiating a "truth" commission with Argentina to re-investigate the 1994 AMIA bombing in Buenos Aires. In the ninth chapter, former Argentine congressman Julian Obiglio and researcher Diego Naveira survey this brazen ploy, and the evolving relationship between Iran and the government of Cristina Fernández de Kirchner in Buenos Aires.

Recent political developments in Latin America and the Middle East have prompted significant changes to Iran's strategy. Growing instability in Venezuela has prompted Iran to reshuffle its regional operations. Meanwhile, the election of a new president in Iran, and the subsequent start of nuclear negotiations with the West, represent a potential game changer for the Islamic Republic, providing it greater international legitimacy—and, potentially, new allies and opportunities in the Americas. In the final two chapters, co-author Ilan Berman and I explore these developments and the policies and strategies that can be employed by the U.S. government and our regional allies in response.

Up to now, the dangers associated with Iran's presence in Latin America have been voiced primarily by U.S. experts. That state of affairs has led some to conclude that the message is alarmist, and out of touch with realities on the ground in the region. The importance of this book, then, is that the analysis it contains does not solely come from U.S. experts, but showcases analysts from Latin America who depict in extensive detail the emerging challenge that Iran poses in their respective home countries. It is a timely reminder that the threat posed by the Islamic Republic is not confined to Israel, or even to the United States. Rather, it is global in nature, and requires a global response.

NOTES

1. Guido Olimpio, "Il Facilitatore che Studia gli Attentati in Sud America, tra gli Obvietti-vi Brasile e Colombia," *Corriere dela Serra* (Milan), May 17, 2012, http://www.corriere.it/esteri/12_maggio_17/allarme-attentati-sud-america-facilitatore_1be4448a-a026-11e1-bef4-97346b368e73.shtml.

2. See, for example, "Annex A, Unclassified Summary of Policy Recommendations," as appended to "Press Release: Duncan Releases Statement on the State Department's Report on Iranian Activity and Influence in the Western Hemisphere," Office of Congressman Jeff Duncan, June 26, 2013.

Chapter One

What Iran Wants in the Americas

Ilan Berman

In October of 2011, the Obama administration went public with news of a new, and significant, terrorist plot that had recently been thwarted by U.S. law enforcement agencies.[1] The scheme detailed by Attorney General Eric Holder and FBI Director Robert Mueller involved an elaborate effort by elements of Iran's clerical army, the Revolutionary Guard Corps, to assassinate Adel al-Jubeir, Saudi Arabia's ambassador to Washington, at a Washington, D.C., restaurant, utilizing members of Mexico's notorious *Los Zetas* drug cartel to carry out the hit.[2]

The foiled October 2011 plot, with its significant connections south of the border, focused attention on what had until then been a largely overlooked political phenomenon: the intrusion of the Islamic Republic into the Western Hemisphere. But while Iran's regional inroads have garnered considerable attention from experts and the press since, the motivations behind them remain poorly understood. This has led some observers to dismiss Iran's activities in Latin America as representing little more than an "axis of annoyance."[3]

Such a characterization, however, understates the significance of Iran's efforts in the Americas—as well as their potential adverse effects on U.S. national security and American interests. That is because Iran's inroads are part of a systematic, long-term strategy on the part of the Islamic Republic to expand its influence and capabilities in the Western Hemisphere. These efforts, moreover, have steadily expanded in recent years. As a result, Iran's strategic presence in Latin America today is significantly greater than it was a decade ago—and it is still growing.

A HISTORY OF VIOLENCE

Iran's intrusion into the region cannot be said to be an entirely new phenomenon. The Islamic Republic has exhibited some level of activity in Latin America since the mid-1980s, when it assisted its chief terrorist proxy, Lebanon's powerful Hezbollah militia, to become entrenched in the so-called "Triple Frontier" where Argentina, Brazil and Paraguay meet.

Hezbollah's regional presence and capabilities were dramatically demonstrated several years later, when it carried out a March 1992 suicide bombing against Israel's embassy in Buenos Aires, Argentina, killing 29 and injuring 242 others. Two years later, in July of 1994, the group struck again, bombing the Argentine-Israel Mutual Association (AMIA) in Buenos Aires. These attacks, which still rank among the most devastating in South American history, led U.S. officials to conclude that Hezbollah had become "the major international terrorist threat" in the region.[4]

Hezbollah is not alone, to be sure. According to U.S. government estimates, no fewer than six Islamic terrorist groups (including al-Qaeda and the Palestinian Hamas movement) are now active in Latin America.[5] Yet Hezbollah is far and away the most prominent—and, arguably, the most capable, thanks largely to its connection with the Islamic Republic. As Alberto Nisman, the Argentine state prosecutor in charge of investigating the 1994 AMIA attacks, has laid out in painstaking detail, Hezbollah's activities in the region were and continue to be facilitated by an extensive network of informal contacts and illicit activities erected by Iranian operatives throughout the Americas.[6]

The Iranian regime's formal outreach to the region, by contrast, is of more recent vintage. It originated as an outgrowth of the "twenty-first century Socialism" championed by Venezuelan strongman Hugo Chávez following his ascension to power in Caracas in 1999. That ideology promoted the pursuit of anti-American alliances, both within the Americas and outside them, as a way of diluting the influence of the United States and erecting an independent regional order.[7] This priority made closer alignment with various radical regimes in the Middle East a logical policy choice for Caracas. And not long thereafter, the 2005 election of Mahmoud Ahmadinejad to the Iranian presidency provided Chávez with a suitable partner in Tehran.

The resulting strategic partnership grew by leaps and bounds in the years that followed. Venezuela emerged as an important source of material assistance for Iran's nuclear program, as well as a vocal diplomatic backer of Iran's will to atomic power. The Chávez regime itself also became a safe haven and source of financial support for Hezbollah.[8] In turn, Iran's feared Revolutionary Guards grew deeply involved in training Venezuela's secret services and police.[9] Economic ties between Caracas and Tehran likewise exploded—expanding from virtually nil in the early 2000s to trade and cooperation agreements worth a potential $20 billion by 2010.[10]

Just as significantly, Venezuela became a "gateway" of sorts for Iran's further economic and diplomatic expansion into the region. Aided by its partnership with Caracas and bolstered by a shared anti-American outlook with other "Bolivarian" countries (such as Bolivia and Ecuador), Iran succeeded in forging significant strategic, economic and political links in the region. It did so along several lines.

BUILDING SUPPORT IN THE AMERICAS

Since the mid-2000s, Iran has invested heavily in political contacts with the Americas on a number of levels. Diplomatically, it has more than doubled its presence in the region over the past decade, increasing its embassies from five in 2005 to eleven today.[11] Iran now boasts an official diplomatic presence in Argentina, Bolivia, Brazil, Chile, Colombia, Cuba, Ecuador, Mexico, Nicaragua, Uruguay and Venezuela.

It likewise has broadened its public diplomacy outreach, launching a dedicated Spanish-language television channel, known as *HispanTV*, in early 2012.[12] *HispanTV* is funded by the Iranian government's official Islamic Republic of Iran Broadcasting company (IRIB), and beams out of Tehran to some fourteen countries in the region.[13] The goal of this effort, according to Iranian officials, is to expand the Iranian regime's "ideological legitimacy" among friendly governments in the region—and to diminish the influence of "dominance seekers," a thinly veiled reference to the United States.[14]

Perhaps most significantly, Iran has engaged in extensive cultural contacts throughout the region. It has done so via numerous formal cultural centers throughout South and Central America, as well as through outreach to the various indigenous populations which represent important bases of political support for regional leaders like Bolivia's Evo Morales, Ecuador's Rafael Correa and Peru's Ollanta Humala.[15] These contacts, and concurrent proselytization activities (known as *daw'ah*), are carried out through a network of "informal ambassadors" operating in the region—a network that was nurtured and trained by Mohsen Rabbani, a former Iranian cultural attaché to Argentina who is alleged to have masterminded the 1994 AMIA attack.[16]

Prior to the start of negotiations between Iran and the P5+1 powers (the United States, United Kingdom, France, Russia, China and Germany) in November 2013, this outreach was intended to shore up support for the Iranian regime's nuclear effort, and to fracture the fragile international consensus concerning the need for sanctions in response to Iranian behavior. But Iran's activism also extends to proselytization activities designed to promote its particular brand of political Islam, and ideological coalition-building intended to make the region more inhospitable to the United States than it is currently. "Iran continues to seek to increase its stature by countering U.S. influence and expanding ties with regional actors while advocating Islamic solidarity," the Pentagon noted in its April 2012 report to Congress on the military power of Iran.[17] Latin America is among the regions where this strategy is being actively implemented.

LEVERAGING LATIN AMERICAN ECONOMIES

Latin America has long functioned as a "support" theater for Iran and its proxies, with money generated through gray and black market activities (ranging from drugs to money laundering) sent back to benefit the Iranian regime or its affiliated groups.[18] With the growth of Iran's strategic partnership with Venezuela, the Chávez regime became part of this network as well. With the active cooperation of Caracas, the Iranian government exploited the Venezuelan financial sector—via joint financial institutions, shell companies and lax banking practices—to continue to access the global economy in recent years despite mounting Western sanctions.[19]

These illicit financial flows have been supplemented by formal trade agreements and contracts between Iran and various regional states. The Iranian regime is estimated to have signed approximately 500 cooperative agreements with regional governments, many of them economic in nature. But, with the notable exception of those concluded with Venezuela, the vast majority of these commitments have yet to materialize. Nevertheless, Iran's overall trade with the region has grown considerably in recent years. In the years between 2000 and 2005, it averaged approximately $1.33 billion annually. As of 2012, this figure had more than doubled, to $3.67 billion.[20]

A QUEST FOR STRATEGIC RESOURCES

Over the past decade, as its strategic programs have matured, the Iranian regime has significantly expanded its efforts to acquire resources for them from abroad. Consequently, since the mid-2000s Iran has become a major speculator in Latin America's resource wealth.

Beginning late last decade, the Islamic Republic commenced mining activities in the uranium-rich Roraima Basin on Venezuela's eastern border, adjacent to Guyana, where it is believed to be involved in the extraction of uranium ore for its nuclear program.[21] More recently, Iran is rumored to have begun prospecting for the same mineral in locations outside of the Bolivia's industrial capital, Santa Cruz, in the country's east.[22] Significantly, the extent of this activity—and whether Iran has actually begun to acquire sizeable quantities of uranium from Latin America—remains a subject of considerable debate among experts and observers, both in the region and in Washington.

More concrete evidence exists of Iran's acquisition of other strategic minerals with potential weapons applications from the region. For example, Iran has become a "partner" in the development of Bolivia's reserves of lithium, a key strategic mineral with applications for nuclear weapons development, pursuant to a formal agreement signed with the Morales government in 2010.[23] Iran is also known to be seeking to acquire at least two other minerals utilized in nuclear work and the production of ballistic missiles: tantalum and thorium.[24]

ERECTING AN ASYMMETRIC NETWORK

Iran's formal presence in the region has been mirrored by an expansion of Iranian covert activities. In its 2010 report to Congress on Iran's military power, the Department of Defense noted that the Qods Force, the elite paramilitary unit of Iran's Revolutionary Guards, is now deeply involved in the Americas, stationing "operatives in foreign embassies, charities and religious/cultural institutions to foster relationships with people, often building on existing socio-economic ties with the well-established Shia Diaspora," and even carrying out "paramilitary operations to support extremists and destabilize unfriendly regimes."[25]

Iran has likewise invested in regional paramilitary infrastructure. Most prominently, it helped establish and subsequently administer the "regional defense school" of the Bolivarian Alliance for the Americas (ALBA), headquartered outside Santa Cruz in eastern Bolivia. Iran is known to have provided at least some of the seed money for the school's construction, and no less senior a figure than Iranian Defense Minister Ahmad Vahidi presided over the school's inauguration in May 2011. Iran—itself an ALBA observer nation—has since played a role in training and indoctrination at the facility.[26]

In parallel with its investments in paramilitary infrastructure, Iran has also forged links with an array of radical groups active in the region, either directly or via Hezbollah. These ties have the potential to significantly augment Iran's capabilities. As then-House Foreign Affairs Committee chairwoman Ileana Ros-Lehtinen (R-FL) noted in 2012, Iran's regional alliances "can pose an immediate threat by giving Iran—directly through the IRGC, the Qods Force, or its proxies like Hezbollah—a platform in the region to carry out attacks against the United States, our interests, and allies."[27]

A FOOTPRINT IN FLUX

Of late, however, Iran's strategic presence in Latin America has undergone considerable change.

Most directly, the core partnership that animated Iran's initial entry into the region in the early 2000s has dissipated. The April 2013 death of Venezuelan President Hugo Chávez following a protracted battle with cancer removed one half of the Iranian regime's most vibrant personal relationship in the region. The end of Mahmoud Ahmadinejad's tenure as Iran's president in June of 2013 has removed the other.

In Venezuela, Nicolas Maduro, Hugo Chávez's handpicked successor as president, has presided over an all-out implosion of the national economy and rapidly rising insecurity since taking office in mid-2013.[28] As a result, even though Maduro—who, as foreign minister, managed his government's contacts with Iran—continues to mimic Chávez's sympathetic attitude toward the Islamic Republic, conventional wisdom holds that his regime no longer possesses either the political stability or economic solvency to serve as Iran's regional anchor.

Conditions within Iran have changed significantly as well. The summer 2013 election of Hassan Rouhani to the Iranian presidency ushered in a new tone in Iranian politics, and facilitated a fresh round of nuclear negotiations between Tehran and the West. As a result of these talks, Iran has to date gained substantial relief from Western economic sanctions.[29] More and more, Iran's previously isolated economy also is benefiting from renewed trade with countries in Europe and Asia.[30] As a result, the importance of Latin America as an economic lifeline for the Iranian regime has diminished at least somewhat.

Given the foregoing, the conventional wisdom in Washington has become that Iran is receding in the region. In its May 2013 report to Congress on the issue, the State Department's Bureau of Western Hemispheric Affairs concluded that the Islamic Republic's regional presence is on the wane—and that as a result Iran no longer constitutes a threat to U.S. regional interests.[31] Such a conclusion, however, is exceedingly premature, for several concrete reasons.

THE PERSISTENCE OF IRAN'S PRESENCE

In hindsight, the year 2012 can be said to have been the "high water" mark for Iran's presence in Latin America, and the Islamic Republic's activities have since receded in both scope and pace. But Iran should nonetheless be considered a significant strategic actor in the region, because along every prong of its outreach to the Americas, the Iranian regime is maintaining, if not expanding, its level of activity. Moreover, a number of political trends—among them Bolivia's recently announced quest for a nuclear capability,[32] the unfolding contest for the post-Chávez leadership of the ALBA bloc of nations, and the controversial peace process now underway in Colombia between the recently re-elected government of Juan Manuel Santos and the Revolutionary Armed Forces of Colombia (FARC)—suggest Iran may have even greater opportunity to influence regional politics in the years ahead then it does currently.

Tehran, for its part, maintains a desire to do so. Hassan Rouhani, Mahmoud Ahmadinejad's successor as Iranian president, has declared that the Islamic Republic is committed to expanding its ties to Latin America,[33] putting to rest speculation that Iran's interest in the Americas was simply a fleeting project of the Ahmadinejad era. In keeping with this continued interest, in May 2014 a high-level parliamentary delegation from Iran embarked upon a Latin American "tour"—an exercise that involved public affirmations of the close bonds and continued strategic convergence between Iran and the ALBA bloc of nations.[34]

As the foregoing suggests, Iran is pursuing a systematic, long-term strategy to expand both its influence and capabilities in the Western Hemisphere. This effort, moreover, continues to be actively engaged in the Iranian regime, irrespective of its unfolding rapprochement with the United States and Europe. As Iran's presence in the region continues to grow, so too does its ability to hold at risk America's regional allies, its interests in the Hemisphere, and even the U.S. homeland itself.

NOTES

1. This chapter is adapted and updated from the author's July 2013 testimony before the House of Representatives Homeland Security Committee Subcommittee on Oversight and Management Efficiency.

2. Charles Savage and Scott Shane, "Iranians Accused of a Plot to Kill Saudis' U.S. Envoy," *New York Times*, October 11, 2011, http://www.nytimes.com/2011/10/12/us/us-accuses-iranians-of-plotting-to-kill-saudi-envoy.html?pagewanted=all (accessed 2014).

3. See Cynthia J. Arnson, Haleh Esfandiari and Adam Stubits, eds. "Iran in Latin America: Threat or 'Axis of Annoyance'?" Woodrow Wilson Center *Reports on the Americas* no. 23, July 2008, http://www.wilsoncenter.org/sites/default/files/Iran_in_LA.pdf (accessed 2014).

4. U.S. Department of State Coordinator for Counterterrorism Phillip Wilcox, Jr., *Testimony before the House of Representatives Committee on International Relations,* September 28, 1995, http://dosfan.lib.uic.edu/ERC/bureaus/lat/1995/950928WilcoxTerrorism.html (accessed 2014).

5. Rex Hudson, *Terror and Organized Crime Groups in the Tri-Border Area (TBA) of South America*, Library of Congress, Federal Research Division, December 2010, http://www.loc.gov/rr/frd/pdf-files/TerrOrgCrime_TBA.pdf (accessed 2014).

6. The English-language translation of Alberto Nisman's indictment is available online at http://www.defenddemocracy.org/stuff/uploads/documents/summary_%2831_pages%29.pdf (accessed 2014).

7. For a detailed discussion, see Jon B. Purdue, *The War of All the People: The Nexus of Latin American Radicalism and Middle Eastern Terrorism* (Dulles, VA: Potomac Books, 2012).

8. Martin Arostengui, "U.S. Ties Caracas to Hezbollah Aid," *Washington Times*, July 7,2008, http://www.washingtontimes.com/news/2008/jul/07/us-ties-caracas-to-hezbollah-aid (accessed 2014).

9. "Iran Using Venezuela To Duck UN Sanctions: Report," *Agence France Presse*, December 21, 2008, http://www.google.com/hostednews/afp/article/ALeqM5h1fferlbgjsi 06XFgTklru3hbatA (accessed 2014).

10. See, for example, Steven Heydemann, "Iran's Alternative Allies," in Robin Wright, ed., *The Iran Primer: Power, Politics and U.S. Policy* (Washington, D.C.: United States Institute of Peace Press, 2010), http://iranprimer.usip.org/resource/irans-alternative-allies (accessed 2014).

11. "Obama Signs Law against Iran's Influence in Latin America," *Agence France Presse*, December 29, 2012, http://www.dailynewsegypt.com/2012/12/29/obama-signs-law-against-irans-influence-in-latin-america (accessed 2014).

12. Hugh Tomlinson, "Tehran Opens 24-hour News TV," *Times of London*, February 1, 2012, http://www.thetimes.co.uk/tto/news/world/middleeast/article3304624.ece (accessed 2014).

13. See "Iran Se Escuchara en Espanol con El Canal Hispan TV," *Correo de Orinoco* (Caracas) July 18, 2011, http://www.correodelorinoco.gob.ve/multipolaridad/iran-se-escuchara-espanol-canal-hispan-tv/ (accessed 2014). A list of countries where HispanTV is broadcast is available online at http://hispantv.com/Distribucion.aspx. Notably, the United States is among those countries where cable providers both accept and distribute the Iranian channel.

14. Ian Black, "Iran to Launch Spanish-Language Television Channel," *Guardian* (London) September 30, 2010, http://www.guardian.co.uk/world/2010/sep/30/iran-spanish-language-television; "Iran Launches Spanish TV Channel," *Associated Press* 2012, http://www.guardian.co.uk/world/2012/jan/31/iran-launches-spanish-tv-channel (accessed 2014).

15. Author's interviews, Quito, Ecuador, May 2012.

16. Joseph Humire, "Iran's Informal Ambassadors to Latin America," *Fox News Latino*, February 18, 2012, http://latino.foxnews.com/latino/politics/2012/02/18/joseph-humire-irans-informal-ambassadors-to-latin-america/ (accessed 2014).

17. Department of Defense, Office of the Secretary of Defense, "Executive Summary: Annual Report on Military Power of Iran," April 2012, http://www.fas.org/man/eprint/dod-iran.pdf (accessed 2014).

18. Hudson, *Terror and Organized Crime Groups in the Tri-Border Area (TBA) of South America*; U.S. Department of Defense, Office of the Secretary of Defense, *Unclassified Report on Military Power of Iran*, April 2010, http://www.iranwatch.org/government/us-dod-reportmiliarypoweriran-0410.pdf (accessed 2014).

19. Norman A. Bailey, "Iran's Venezuelan Gateway," American Foreign Policy Council *Iran Strategy Brief* no. 5, February 2012, http://www.afpc.org/files/getContentPostAttachment/ 213 (accessed 2014).

20. Figures derived from the International Monetary Fund's Direction of Trade Statistics database. (Compilation in author's collection.)

21. Stephen Johnson, *Iran's Influence in the Americas* (Washington, D.C.: Center for Strategic and International Studies, March 2012), xiv, http://csis.org/files/publication/120312__ Johnson_Iran percent27sInfluence_web.pdf (accessed 2014).

22. Author's interviews, La Paz and Santa Cruz, Bolivia, January–February 2012.

23. "Iran 'Partner' in the Industrialization of Bolivia's Lithium Reserves," *MercoPress*, October 30, 2010, http://en.mercopress.com/2010/10/30/iran-partner-in-the-industrialization-of-bolivia-s-lithium-reserves (accessed 2014).

24. Author's interviews in Chile, Bolivia and Argentina, January–February 2012.

25. U.S. Department of Defense, *Unclassified Report on Military Power of Iran*, April 2010.

26. Purdue, *The War of All the People*, 154–156.

27. Ileana Ros-Lehtinen, Opening statement before House Foreign Affairs Committee hearing on "Ahmadinejad's Tour of Tyrants and Iran's Agenda in the Western Hemisphere,"

February 2, 2012. Reproduced at http://interamericansecuritywatch.com/iran%E2%80%99s-ties-in-latin-american-region-pose-threat-to-u-s-security-ros-lehtinen-says-at-hearing/ (accessed 2014).

28. See, for example, James Hider, "Toilet Paper Running out as Venezuela's Economy Goes Down the Pan," *Times of London*, May 17, 2013, http://www.thetimes.co.uk/tto/news/world/americas/article3766919.ece (accessed 2014).

29. Exactly how much sanctions relief Iran has obtained to date remains the subject of some debate. The Obama administration has projected that the relief will total some $7 billion. However, observers suggest that the actual sum of the economic windfall received by Iran will be substantially greater: $20 million, or higher. See Adam Credo, "Iran to Get 'More Than $20B' in Sanctions Relief; Accuracy of Obama Promise Questioned," *Washington Times*, February 14, 2014, http://www.washingtontimes.com/news/2014/feb/14/iran-get-more-20b-sanctions-relief-accuracy-obama-/?page=all (accessed 2014).

30. "Asia's Iran Oil Buys Start to Rise After Nuclear Deal," *Reuters*, March 1, 2014, http://www.dailytimes.com.pk/business/01-Mar-2014/asia-s-iran-oil-buys-start-to-rise-after-nuclear-deal (accessed 2014).

31. See, for example, Guy Taylor, "State Secrets: Kerry's Department Downplays Iran's Role in Latin America; Likely to Anger Congress," *Washington Times*, June 23, 2013, http://www.washingtontimes.com/news/2013/jun/23/state-department-downplays-iran-role-in-latin-amer/?page=all (accessed 2014).

32. "Bolivia 'to Build First Nuclear Reactor,'" *BBC*, January 22, 2014, http://www.bbc.com/news/world-latin-america-25855041 (accessed 2014).

33. See, for example, "Iran Firm to Boost Ties with Latin America: Rouhani," *PressTV* (Tehran) February 10, 2014, http://www.presstv.com/detail/2014/02/10/350081/iran-vows-close-ties-with-latam-mexico/ (accessed 2014).

34. "Iranian MPs Leave Tehran for Tour of Latin America," *FARS* (Tehran) May 26, 2014, http://english.farsnews.com/newstext.aspx?nn=13930305001318 (accessed 2014).

Chapter Two

A Marriage of Radical Ideologies

Jon B. Perdue

When considering what drives men and women to turn themselves into martyrs for a radical cause, we often look to the tenets of their religion or ideology for the offending passages that could be so lyrically powerful as to drive them to their own destruction. But we may be looking in vain. The empirical evidence shows that it is militancy itself, rather than the edifying proverbs of some religious text or political manifesto that propels extremists to sacrifice themselves.

Whether one puts life at risk for *La Revolución* or the *Jihad*, the common motivation can be found in their common cause. While the ideological marriage of Middle Eastern Islamic extremism and Latin American "Twenty-first Century Socialism" has been most evident in recent years in the relationship between the late Venezuelan president Hugo Chávez and former Iranian president Mahmoud Ahmadinejad, its roots run far deeper, and stretch further back in time.

THE COURTSHIP BEGINS

When the Ayatollah Ruhollah Khomeini came to power in the 1979 Iranian Revolution, the fervor of the moment produced an ideological shift from Marxist to Khomeinist revolutionary thinking. Journalist Amir Taheri catalogued the instant conversions of many erstwhile Marxists and Maoists to radical Islamic ideology:

> The members of the Soviet-created Communists of the Tudeh (Masses) Party replaced their portraits of Marx and Lenin with those of Ali Ibn Abi-Talib and Hussein Ibn Ali, the first and third imams of Shiism. Their chief ideologist, the octogenarian Ihsan Tabari, even wrote a book to prove that Ali had been the

11

true founder of 'Socialism.' Then there were the People's Mujahedin, a Marx-ist-Islamist terrorist organization that specialized in robbing banks and killing policemen. Alongside them were two versions of another terror group, the so-called People's Fedayeen Guerrillas, one pro-Moscow, the other pro-Peking. There were, as well, the Trotskyites, the Spartacists, the Guevarists and count-less other leftist terrorist gangs with names like 'Storm,' 'Thunder,' 'Workers' Banner' and 'Red Star.'[1]

This shift would continue throughout the 1980s, as the Soviet Union lost favor with many in the Middle East due to its actions in Afghanistan. When the Soviet Union finally imploded in January of 1989, Iran's Khomeini sent a letter to Soviet Premier Mikhail Gorbachev suggesting that he "seriously . . . study and conduct research into Islam," and "not fall into the prison of the West and the Great Satan." Khomeini, seeing the Iranian revolution as the natural successor to Soviet Communism, declared: "I openly announce that the Islamic Republic of Iran, as the greatest and most powerful base of the Islamic world, can easily help fill up the ideological vacuum of your sys-tem."[2]

Two decades later, a similar entreaty was made when the Iranian regime invited the children of Ernesto "Che" Guevara, the infamous Argentine ideo-logue, to Tehran to attend a conference designed to showcase "the common goals" of Islamist radicals and the Socialist left. The only friction between the two factions came when Hajj Saeed Qassemi, the coordinator of the conference claimed that Che Guevara had only feigned his atheism, and was "a truly religious man who believed in God and hated communism and the Soviet Union." Guevara's daughter, Aleida, clarified her objection by stating what many already suspected: "My father never met God." This was the extent of the disagreement.

Subsequent speakers at the conference, from both sides, agreed that their common mission was to attack America "everywhere and all the time," ac-cording to Mortaza Firuzabadi, a radical Khomeinist. The tone of the confer-ence was one of unity among revolutionary movements worldwide, and Firu-zabadi assured the assembled audience that the coalition of Islamists and far-left radicals would defeat the Great Satan because they do not fear death, whereas the "Americans are scared of dying."

Qassemi returned to the stage towards the end of the conference to reiter-ate what Khomeini had communicated to Gorbachev two decades before: "The Soviet Union is gone. The leadership of the downtrodden has passed to our Islamic Republic. Those who wish to destroy America must understand this reality."[3] The message was clear: Iran's ayatollahs aimed to fill the void left by the fall of the Soviet Union, and lead other socialist countries in the continuing fight against Western powers. Thus, they turned to Latin Ameri-ca.

LATIN AMERICA: THE NEW MECCA FOR TERRORISTS

Though the cultures in Latin America and Iran could not be more antithetical, the mullahs of Iran found that their pejorative attitudes toward women and modernity in general would be overlooked as long as they adopted the anti-American political rhetoric of the international left. The seeds of this unlikely cross-cultural relationship had long ago been planted when Fidel Castro of Cuba and Muammar Qaddafi of Libya set up *Al Mathaba*, a joint propaganda apparatus based in Havana and Tripoli that would coordinate anti-American messaging throughout both hemispheres.[4]

Al Mathaba, also known as the Anti-Imperialism Center (AIC), was established in 1982 to aid "anti-imperialist" forces worldwide, mostly involving the left-wing guerrilla movements that were most active in Europe, the Middle East and Latin America at the time. It would later evolve to become a logistics coordination center for directly assisting worldwide terrorist movements. Until President Ronald Reagan called for an airstrike on Tripoli in 1986, *Al Mathaba* served to facilitate money and supply transfers via Libya's embassies and consulates throughout the world. It was this model that Iran would later replicate when deciding to use its embassies to facilitate the spread of its revolution throughout Latin America.

In 1982, the Iranian regime held a meeting in Tehran in which it was decided that it would use proxy terrorist groups to export its revolution, facilitated by its embassies and mosques around the world. Within a few months of the meeting, the regime sent Iranian cleric Mohsen Rabbani as a commercial attaché to Argentina. Rabbani, who was supposedly sent to inspect livestock, had a more subversive purpose in mind, stating:

> According to our Islamic point of view, Latin America is for us and the international world, a virgin area that unfortunately, till now, its huge potential has not been taken into account by the Islamic people of Iran. (. . .) we have a solid support against the imperialism and Zionism intrigues, being an important aid in favor of our presence in the area.[5]

Rabbani's assertion was not without foundation. From the 1970s, Palestinian terrorists had been training Latin American guerrillas in terrorist tactics. A CIA National Intelligence Estimate at the time stated that, "El Salvador is the most prominent current target of the Palestinians in Latin America. During 1980, Palestinians trained some 200 Salvadoran rebels in Lebanon."[6] In 1985, when terrorist activity in El Salvador had cooled and Nicaragua became the flashpoint, the *Miami Herald* reported that a diverse group of terrorists were congregating in Managua, under the aegis of the left-wing Sandinista regime.[7] The subsequent fall of the Sandinista regime and the pressure exerted by the Reagan administration throughout the region would scatter these actors, until Hugo Chávez came to power in Venezuela in 1999 and once again offered a safe haven.

Yet, the extent to which the Chávez regime was collaborating with terrorist groups was mostly a matter of speculation until Spanish author Antonio Salas published *El Palestino* (*The Palestinian*) in 2010, a firsthand chronicle of his infiltration into Venezuela's terrorist underground. Salas (the author's *nom de plume*) was already known for infiltrating a human trafficking organization and a gang of skinheads in Europe. His book on Venezuela's terrorist infiltration revealed that there were as many as six terrorist training camps, mostly run by Venezuelan military officers, spread around the capital city of Caracas and Margarita Island off their Caribbean coast. However, Salas' strangest discovery, according to Giles Tremlett of London's *Guardian* newspaper, was "the willingness of different extremist groups to blindly embrace the varied causes of others, even when they had nothing to do with one another."[8]

ARGENTINA AS THE INTELLECTUAL HUB FOR ISLAMIC EXTREMISM

This merging of radical-right and radical-left forces is perhaps nowhere more pronounced than in Argentina, where the Iranian regime carried out one of the largest terrorist attacks in the hemisphere prior to 9/11, bombing the Israeli Embassy in 1992 and the AMIA Jewish community center in 1994. Decades before these attacks, Argentine politics featured its own admixture of radical ideologies—an intellectual morass that provided fertile soil for Islamic extremism to take root once Rabbani touched down in Buenos Aires.

Argentina's affinity for radical ideologies goes back to the cult of personality built by Juan Peron. His eponymous ideology, "Peronism," was based on an eclectic mix of the worst elements of far-right nationalism and far-left collectivism. Peron developed his ideology while in exile in Spain, where he developed close relationships with Jean-Francois Thiriart and Otto "Scarface" Skorzeny.

The former, Thiriart, was a Belgian that moved from the radical left in his early years to the far right later in life, and served as an advisor to the PLO's Fatah faction in the 1970s.[9] The latter, Skorzeny, was a notorious Nazi commando who planned and executed the prison break of Fascist dictator Benito Mussolini in 1943. Once the Nazi regime fell, Skorzeny fled to Egypt and served under their second president, Gamal Abdel Nasser.[10] Both Skorzeny and Thiriart had a profound effect on further radicalizing Peron's ideology, and introduced him to Islamic extremism.

It is upon this backdrop that Argentina's current president, Cristina Kirchner—herself a former radical-left militant and self proclaimed Peronist—

could plausibly make the statement: "When the (conservative) right says you are Marxist and the alleged revolutionary left calls you right-wing, it means you are a consummate Peronist."[11] This terrain of eclectic ideologies welcomed Iran's emissary, Mohsen Rabbani, who in 1991 stood before a group of Shi'ite Muslims and radical right-wing Argentine activists and stated openly, "Israel must disappear from the face of the Earth," to universal applause.[12]

Just one year after Rabbani's speech, the Iranians would bomb the Israeli Embassy, and two years thereafter, the AMIA Jewish community center. The Iranian presence would recede for nearly a decade afterward, until Hugo Chávez began courting the Iranian regime to form an anti-American alliance.

While Chávez was known as merely a left-wing ideologue, his background betrays a more complicated ideology. To understand this, it is important to look at Chávez's ideological mentor, the Argentine sociologist Norberto Ceresole, whose influence helped shape his worldview. Ceresole got his start with the left wing militias that supported Juan Peron, and eventually ended up in Venezuela in 1994, about the time that Chávez was getting out of prison for his 1992 coup attempt. The president of Venezuela at the time, Rafael Caldera, banished Ceresole from the country a year later because of his ties to Islamist terrorists. Once Chávez won the presidency in 1998, Ceresole returned. Upon his return, Ceresole wrote a paean to Chávez titled, *"Caudillo, Ejercito, Pueblo"* (*"Leader, Army, People"*), in which the first chapter, "The Jewish Question and the State of Israel," lays the blame for his exile, and most of the world's problems, on Israel and the international Jewish community.[13]

Ceresole, after claiming that the Jews use the "myth" of the Holocaust to control the world, declared, "I am not anti-Semitic nor a neo-Nazi . . . I am a critic of the State of Israel and of the international Jewish organizations, to which I have devoted my last few books." Ceresole once proposed to Chávez the creation of an Office of Strategic Intelligence, an intelligence operation that would be financed by donations from Hezbollah. Ceresole had set up a similar operation previously in Madrid, but he died in 2003 before he could do the same in Venezuela.[14] Nevertheless, Ceresole's anti-Semitic ideology made its mark on Latin America as Chávez brought his mentor's influence to the world stage through his cooperation with Islamic extremists and hostile treatment of the United States, Israel, and his own Jewish community in Venezuela.

CHAVEZ'S ANTI-SEMITIC SENTIMENTS

Upon Mahmoud Ahmadinejad's election as President of Iran in 2005, a true strategic partnership emerged between Tehran and Caracas. And as relations

between Chávez and Ahmadinejad deepened, so did the former's anti-Semitic and anti-Israel bias. Chávez took the opportunity of a 2005 speech about
Christopher Columbus's discovery of the Americas, for example, to compare
the oppression suffered by Venezuela's indigenous population under the con-
quistadors to the plight of the Palestinians. He told the crowd that Venezuela's indigenous inhabitants had been "murdered in their land" by "governments, economic sectors, and the large landed estates," and concluded with
"you were expelled from your homeland, like the heroic Palestinian people."[15]

Chávez became an overnight hero in the Middle East when he was the
first head of state to condemn Israel after it retaliated in 2006 against Hezbollah rocket attacks. On his weekly radio show, Chávez said that Israel was
"going mad and inflicting on the people of Palestine and Lebanon the same
thing they have criticized, and with reason: the Holocaust. But this is a new
Holocaust." He went on to describe the "new Holocaust" as a plot by the
United States, which he called a "terrorist country," that would not "allow
the United Nations Security Council to make a decision to halt the genocide
Israel is committing against the Palestinian and Lebanese people."[16]

As Hezbollah continued its war against Israel in 2006, Chávez's rhetoric
became even more aggressive. In a July 28, 2006, interview with *Al Jazeera*,
Chávez declared:

> The aggression against Palestine and Lebanon is an aggression against us as
> well. It is an unjustified aggression. It is a fascist aggression, much like Hit-
> ler . . . Israel is right in criticizing Hitler and the hostility against Jews, we do
> too, but they are doing the same thing that Hitler did to the Jews. They are
> killing innocent children, entire families. They destroyed the legitimate
> government of Palestine, they destroyed the multi-year effort of the road to-
> wards peace, looking for a Palestinian state, and now they are targeting Leba-
> non and have destroyed half of Lebanon . . . Behind the hostilities perpetrated
> by Israel is the hand of the U.S. The worst menace that has the future of
> humanity is the U.S. Empire and one of its instruments of aggression is in the
> State of Israel. This plan was prepared in detail a long time ago and it was
> planned in the Pentagon; only that Israel is the executor.[17]

Chávez's radicalism found other expression as well. Later that year, after
he had called President George W. Bush "the devil" in his address to the
United Nations, Chávez sent a reported $1 million to have posters printed of
himself with Hezbollah chief Hassan Nasrallah. One poster, placed on a
bridge that had been hit by Israeli air strikes, showed Chávez and Nasrallah
together and touted a petition to offer thanks to Chávez for his support. The
poster also quoted Nasrallah hailing, "our coalition from Gaza to Beirut, to
Damascus, to Tehran, and with our brother Chávez."[18]

This type of rhetoric would escalate for more than two years, and on January 22, 2009, it would turn to action in Venezuela, when a Sephardic synagogue was broken into and vandalized. The vandals destroyed Torah scrolls and painted anti-Semitic graffiti on the walls warning of death to Venezuela's small Jewish population. Though Chávez offered a perfunctory, one-line condemnation of the attack, he had spent the weeks before stirring up his supporters to condemn Israel's retaliatory response in Gaza, which he referred to as a "genocidal holocaust against the Palestinian people."[19]

Chávez had already declared Israel's ambassador *persona non grata* and demanded criminal prosecution of both Israel's president and U.S. president George W. Bush for mass murder. Shortly thereafter, one of the many state-sponsored websites called for a boycott of Venezuela's Jewish community, along with a protest against the Israeli embassy and Jewish synagogues. It also called for kicking all Jews out of Venezuela.

The toxic climate created by Chávez had a pronounced effect. According to a 2007 report, up to a fifth of Venezuela's 20,000 Jews had emigrated after Chávez's anti-Semitic rhetoric reached the point where it could be perceived by his followers as an incitement to violence. All told, from Chávez's inauguration in January 1999 until November 2010, over half of Venezuela's Jewish population left the country.[20]

THE MARRIAGE CONTINUES

On the first anniversary of Chávez's death, the Syrian regime dedicated a park on the campus of Damascus University to the Venezuelan *caudillo*. In remarks to journalists, Venezuela's ambassador to Syria Imad Saab said: "Chávez wanted, through his visits to friendly countries around the world, to unify the efforts of the anti-imperialist countries."[21]

This legacy has endured. Shortly before his passing, Hugo Chávez declared that the ideological marriage of radical Islam and radical leftism would actually save the world:

> Our calling is to play a key role in freeing the world (by fighting) against
> imperialism, against capitalist and neoliberal hegemony that today threatens
> the survival of the human race . . . Arab civilization and our civilization, the
> Latin American one, are being summoned in this new century to play the
> fundamental role of liberating the world, saving the world from the imperial-
> ism and capitalist hegemony that threaten the human species.[22]

Chávez maintained a coterie of like-minded followers in his government who utilized similar anti-Semitic, anti-Western rhetoric. Tarek William Saab, a Lebanese-Venezuelan politician and leader of Chávez's Fifth Republic Movement (MVR), called himself a "human rights activist," having studied human rights law at the Central University of Venezuela.[23] But Tareck Saab (who is the cousin of Imad Saab) was denied a visa to enter the United States, which he admitted was because a U.S. State Department report had identified him as "an individual linked to international subversion."[24] Venezuelan newspaper *El Nacional* reported, however, that Saab's visa was denied because he allegedly disrupted an ongoing legal process against three Arab members of Hezbollah that were suspects in the 1994 AMIA bombing in Buenos Aires. The three had reportedly traveled from Colombia to Margarita Island in November 1999 and were arrested by the Venezuelan military on July 2002, but subsequently released.[25]

Aside from Saab, Chávez filled his cabinet with Venezuelans of Islamic heritage, and provided them with privileged positions of power within the government. Individuals such as the former Minister of Interior, Tareck El Aissami, Venezuelan diplomat Ghazi Nassereddine, and military commander Aref Richani Jimenez, all of either Syrian or Lebanese descent, parroted Chávez's anti-Semitic rhetoric within their respective areas of authority.

Since his passing, Chávez's allies in the region have continued the rhetoric and close relationship with the Middle East. Bolivia's Evo Morales established a close relationship with Iran and has hosted several visits of high-ranking Iranian officials in recent years, most recently in June 2014 for the G77 Summit in Santa Cruz. Moreover, a week after Venezuela cut diplomatic relations with Israel in 2009, Bolivia followed suit, expelling Israel's diplomats in protest over its military offensive in Gaza. Ecuador's Rafael Correa has tried to replace Chávez as Latin America's welcoming committee to Middle Eastern radicals, furthering ties with both Syria and Iran. Most recently, in May 2014, Correa welcomed an "Iran-Ecuador parliamentary friendship group," which traveled to Quito to meet with members of his government.[26] And in Venezuela, Chávez's hand-picked successor, Nicolas Maduro, despite claiming Jewish ancestry, has kept up the anti-Israel rhetoric, saying that Venezuela under his presidency would continue to fight against the "repressive state of Israel."[27]

While many speculated that the death of Hugo Chávez and the exit of Mahmoud Ahmadinejad would mean the end of the East-West radical alliance, it has continued apace, underscoring the fact that it is militancy itself, rather than ideological kinship or personality cults, which keeps the marriage intact.

NOTES

1. Amir Taheri, "Tehran Tyranny's 25th," *New York Post*, February 10, 2004, http://www.benadorassociates.com/article/1835.

2. Daniel Pipes, *Militant Islam Reaches America* (W.W. Norton & Co., 2003), 9.

3. Amir Taheri, "Tehran's Price for Solidarity," *New York Post*, October 12, 2007.

4. Douglas Farah, "Harvard for Tyrants—How Muammar al-Qaddafi Taught a Generation of Bad Guys," *Foreign Policy*, March 4, 2011, http://www.foreignpolicy.com/articles/2011/03/04/harvard_for_tyrants.

5. Marcelo Martinez Burgos and Alberto Nisman, "AMIA Case," Investigations Unit of the Office of the Attorney General, 2006, pg. 9, http://www.peaceandtolerance.org/docs/nismanindict.pdf.

6. "Soviet Support for International Terrorism and Revolutionary Violence," CIA Special National Intelligence Estimate, released under CIA Historical Review Program, February 28, 1994, pg. 13, http://www.foia.cia.gov/sites/default/files/document_conversions/89801/DOC_0000272980.pdf.

7. "Sandinistas Attract a Who's Who of Terrorists," *Miami Herald*, March 3, 1985.

8. Giles Tremlett, "Carlos the Jackal was my Friend," *Guardian* (London), October 10, 2010, http://www.guardian.co.uk/world/2010/oct/10/carlos-jackal-was-my-friend.

9. Walter Laqueur, *Fascism: Past, Present, Future* (Oxford: Oxford University Press, 1997), 93.

10. Martin Lee, *The Beast Reawakens* (Little, Brown & Co., 1997), 177.

11. "The Lady Out of Control: Appeals to 'Nazi, Mengele and Anti Semitism' to Attack the Media," MercoPress, March 14, 2012, http://en.mercopress.com/2012/03/14/the-lady-out-of-control-appeals-to-nazi-mengele-and-anti-semitism-to-attack-the-media.

12. Tracy Wilkinson, "Hezbollah: The Latin Connection," *Los Angeles Times*, August 4, 1994, http://articles.latimes.com/1994-08-04/news/mn-23412_1_porous-borders.

13. Travis Pantin, "Hugo Chávez's Jewish Problem," *Commentary*, July/August 2008, http://www.commentarymagazine.com/viewarticle.cfm/hugo-ch-vez-s-jewish-problem-11455.

14. Alberto Garrido, "Vida y Muerte De Ceresole," *El Universal*, May 3, 2005.

15. Pantin, "Hugo Chávez's Jewish Problem."

16. Daniel Shoer-Roth, "Uproar: Chávez Equates Nazis, Israelis," *Miami Herald*, August 9, 2006.

17. Anti-Defamation League, "The Chávez Regime: Fostering Anti-Semitism and Supporting Radical Islam Chávez's Allies," November 6, 2006.

18. "Hezbollah Adopts Chávez as Hero," *Agence France Presse*, September 21, 2006.

19. Michael Rowan and Douglas E. Schoen, "Hugo Chávez and anti-Semitism," *Forbes*, February 15, 2009.

20. Shlomo Papirblat, "In Venezuela, Remarks Like 'Hitler Didn't Finish the Job' Are Routine," *Ha'aretz* (Tel Aviv), November 20, 2010.

21. "Park in Damascus University Named after Chávez on His First Death Anniversary," *Islamic Invitation Turkey*, February 25, 2014, http://www.islamicinvitationturkey.com/2014/02/25/park-in-damascus-university-named-after-Chávez-on-his-first-death-anniversary/.

22. "Hosting Syrian leader, Chávez hails anti-Capitalism," *Associated Press*, June 27, 2010, http://www.pressherald.com/2010/06/27/hosting-syrian-leader-Chávez-hails-anti-capitalism_2010-06-27/.

23. "Tarek William Saab en La BitBlioteca," http://www.analitica.com/Bitblio/tarek/.

24. "Tarek Saab solicitará reunión a embajador de Estados Unidos," *El Universal* (Caracas), October 3, 2002, http://buscador.eluniversal.com/2002/10/03/pol_art_03106EE.shtml.

25. Tel Aviv University Stephen Roth Institute, "Anti-Semitism and Racism: Venezuela 2002–2003," n.d., http://www.tau.ac.il/Anti-Semitism/asw2002-3/venezuela.htm.

26. "Iranian MPs Leave Tehran for Tour of Latin America," FARS, May 26, 2014, http://english.farsnews.com/newstext.aspx?nn=13930305001318.

27. Elad Benari, "Maduro: I'm Not Anti-Semitic; My Grandparents Were Jewish," Arutz Sheva, May 21, 2013, http://www.israelnationalnews.com/News/News.aspx/168163#.U6EH27HrQ54.

Chapter Three

The ALBA

Iran's Gateway

Joel Hirst

In order to understand Iran's growing presence in Latin America, it is important to first take note of the regional environment that has allowed it to flourish. For the past decade, much of Latin America has been in the throes of a "Bolivarian revolution" sponsored by Venezuela and Cuba. This revolution has challenged the Western world's system of rule of law and representative democracy, and seeks to replace it with a new authoritarian model of governance. The purpose of this model is to establish a "new world order"—one in which Latin America's transformation is simply one chapter of a global revolution. Ostensibly, Iran's Islamic revolution is another such chapter.[1]

Iran's penetration into Latin America is of strategic importance to the Islamic Republic as it attempts to build diplomatic allies, launder sanctioned money, and position its Revolutionary Guards and terrorist proxies to attack Western targets. Many analysts have written about Iran's motivations for engaging countries in the region.[2] However, most have disregarded the flip side of this coin: namely, what specific countries in Latin America gain from their relationship with Iran and with Iranian proxies such as Hezbollah. In order to understand these motivations, it is essential to first survey the geopolitical ramifications of the *Vene-Cuba* political power project known as the Bolivarian Alliance for the Peoples of our America, or ALBA.

WHAT IS ALBA?

In December 2004, Venezuelan President Hugo Chávez and Cuban President Fidel Castro signed a 12-point agreement creating the Bolivarian Alternative of the Americas.[3] Following his election in 1998, Chávez spent the next five years systematically consolidating power. By 2003, he had re-written the constitution, defeated an attempted coup, nationalized several industries, and won a recall referendum. The Venezuelan opposition was completely dismantled and Chávez then had both the ability and the opportunity to embark unencumbered upon his international agenda.

The Bolivarian Alternative (which quickly became the Bolivarian Alliance for the Peoples of Our America, or ALBA) was initially presented as an alternative to the Free Trade Agreement of the Americas (FTAA), an agreement first envisioned by the Clinton administration (before it was discarded in favor of NAFTA) and then enthusiastically championed by President George W. Bush. Early on, it faced many challenges, due largely to heavy reliance on Venezuelan oil largesse. Most sitting Latin American leaders were not keen on bringing themselves under the influence of Chávez and his Bolivarian project. But as time passed and Chávez invested important economic and political resources in the alliance (by some estimates, more than $60 billion[4]), his efforts began to bear fruit.

Initially, Chávez was able to groom Evo Morales as the next President of Bolivia by providing political and financial support for him during a coca-growers strike in 2002. That support positioned Morales as the main opposition to Bolivia's established order, heralding the end of the country's short-lived experiment with republican democracy. Chávez again supported Morales during his presidential campaign in 2005, which resulted in Evo becoming the first Bolivian president since 1982 to win a majority of the national vote. Shortly thereafter, again through significant financial and political support, Chávez facilitated Daniel Ortega's return to the presidency of Nicaragua, and brought an easily influenced Manuel Zelaya of Honduras into the Bolivarian fold. This was followed by support for Rafael Correa in his bid to win the presidency of Ecuador, bringing that country into his regional alliance as well. And although Argentina is not an official member of ALBA, most observers and analysts consider it to be a de-facto one, insofar as its authoritarian behavior and recent populist policies correspond closely with the ALBA agenda.

Detractors will point out that Chávez only had success in poorer, smaller countries with less efficient economies. This is not entirely true, however. As the following table outlines, ALBA currently has a collective population of close to 70 million individuals, an economy of almost $700 billion and a territory spanning across 2.5 million square kilometers. If Argentina is included in this mix, then ALBA becomes larger than Mexico and rivals Brazil.

Moreover, ALBA has a bank (based in Caracas), a virtual currency (the SUCRE), and a regional television station (TELESUR) that is more important than CNN in some countries, as well as a satellite and underwater fiber-optic cable connected to Cuba. Collectively, the bloc has sixteen Grand National projects in the works, encompassing agriculture, tourism, medicine and other arenas. Every two years, more than 30 nations participate in Olympic-style ALBA games hosted by member states. Additionally, they share a medical school, movie studios, book contests, radio stations, wire services, and hundreds of "social movements" across the region. ALBA charity programs provide eye operations to millions, and—with Venezuelan support—tens of thousands of Cuban doctors, trainers, and intelligence agents are on the move throughout the continent for the first time since the height of the Cold War.

Beyond its socio-economic and psychological impact, ALBA has dominated the political discourse of Latin America for more than a decade. It has held more than twenty summits, and has consistently set the agenda at the Organization of American States while redirecting the latter's influence in the region. ALBA has delayed potential democratic transition in Cuba, frozen multilateral discussions on topics as far ranging as drugs, terrorism, and even climate change, and has led to a degree of regional backsliding on democracy.

Table 3.1.   ALBA by the numbers

Country	Size per square km	Population	GDP (in USD millions)	Date Joined
Antigua & Barbuda	442	85,632	1,522	2009 Jun 24
Bolivia	1,098,581	9,775,246	45,560	2006 Apr 29
Cuba	110,860	11,451,652	110,000	2004 Dec 14
Dominica	751	72,660	744	2008 Jan 20
Ecuador	283,561	14,573,101	108,800	2009 Jun 24
Nicaragua	130,370	5,891,199	16,510	2007 Feb 23
St. Vincent & Grenadines	389	104,574	1,069	2009 Jun 24
Venezuela	912,050	26,814,843	349,300	2004 Dec 14
ALBA Totals:	*2,537,004*	*68,768,907*	*633,505*	

Non-voting Observer Nations: Haiti, Iran, Syria, and Suriname

Yet surprisingly little has been written to date on the topic of ALBA and its strategic importance. Most analysts have tended to treat the organization as strictly a trade arrangement, and are thus frustrated to find that there are no treaties, bylaws, or agreements that would allow them to understand its activities in the traditional sense. As a result, many fail to see ALBA for what it is and for what it describes itself to be: a revolutionary plan to create a regional bloc under Venezuelan and Cuban influence, and to curb U.S. influence in the hopes of bringing about a new, post-American world order.

The idea is not new. The creation of the *Patria Grande*, an idea often alluded to by ALBA leaders and officials, refers to eighteenth-century political leader Simon Bolivar's dream of a Latin American confederation through what he called the Panama Congress: a bloc united in opposition to the United States and Spain. But Bolivar's plan fell short of success, and he had to content himself with only a *Gran Colombia*—a smaller nation under his control comprised only of Ecuador, Colombia, Venezuela, Panama and parts of Costa Rica. Yet even this project fragmented toward the end of Bolivar's life. Over the past decade, the dream of Hugo Chávez was not only to rebuild *Gran Colombia* but to also succeed where Bolivar failed and create a leftist Latin American confederation beholden to Venezuela and Cuba.

DRUGS AND THUGS: THE NEXUS BETWEEN ALBA AND IRAN

ALBA can be best analyzed by comparing it to an onion. Peeling away the first layer reveals the true political nature of this proxy power project, and peeling away the second layer reveals the nefarious activities that prop up the alliance. Within this last layer lies the true focus of the Bolivarian Alliance— the use of non-state actors and transnational organized crime as the ways and means to accomplish its stated ends.

In 2006, President Chávez officially changed his military doctrine from conventional to asymmetric warfare. In keeping with the subversive nature of his regional plan, he believed that sooner or later he would run afoul of some international actor (ostensibly the United States) and thus needed to prepare for an eventual military attack. Having watched the effectiveness of the Iraqi insurgents and the Taliban, and by learning from his close relationship with notorious terrorist Illich Ramirez Sanchez (also known as Carlos the Jackal), he sought the support of Iran and Hezbollah to train and advise his military. Most conspicuously, this resulted in the Iranian bankrolling of an ALBA military training school located near Santa Cruz, Bolivia, and the establishment of Hezbollah training centers in other countries throughout the region.

Iran is not the only nefarious actor in this regard. A common tactic associated with asymmetric warfare is terrorism, and Venezuela's entrance into this murky world has allowed Hezbollah to plan, fundraise, train, coordinate, and carry out operations, mostly fundraising and intelligence collection.[5]

By exploiting these same avenues, organized crime has begun to flourish in the region as well. Colombia's FARC guerrillas, for example, have a long history of drug-running and money laundering, and currently use Venezuela not only as a base of operations but also as a location to transit drugs and other illicit products. The peace process between the Government of Colombia and the FARC has not changed this calculus, but only provided political cover for the group's ongoing illict activities. Iranian terror proxy Hezbollah is similarly known to be deeply involved in the regional drug trade, using the Tri-Border Area at the intersection of Argentina, Paraguay and Brazil as a major base of commercial operations. Over time, several cases have linked Hezbollah to major drug trafficking organizations in the region. Most notable is the widely-known case of Ayman Joumaa, a Lebanese-Colombian who established a vast money-laundering network to move multi-ton shipments of cocaine from Mexico and Colombia to the Middle East, raising tens of millions of dollars on behalf of Hezbollah.[6]

ALBA nations have gotten in on this act as well. According to the United Nations, Bolivia recently achieved the dubious distinction of becoming the world's second-largest cocaine producer.[7] Ecuador is allegedly an increasingly important money-laundering hub for a variety of non-state and rogue actors, due to its dollarized economy. Venezuela's government is similarly complicit; the U.S. Treasury Department's Office of Foreign Asset Control has blacklisted eight current and former members of the Venezuelan government for terror-related and criminal activity.[8] Meanwhile, according to testimony of former Venezuelan judge Aponte Aponte, who has sought refuge in the United States, the largest drug cartel in Venezuela, the Cartel of the Suns, allegedly operates out of military installations and uses military equipment to facilitate drug running.[9]

The growing criminal nature of the ALBA alliance does not just benefit Iran's asymmetric activities in Latin America. It also provides criminal safe haven to Iran's more nefarious actors and actions in the region.

IRAN'S MOTIVATIONS

Against this backdrop, the rationale behind the proximity of ALBA nations to Iran becomes clearer. Iran's motivations, however, are less apparent.

At first glance there would seem to be little in terms of practical policy interests that bind Iran to ALBA. Iran is an energy competitor with ALBA nations, rather than a natural trading partner for them. Both the collective economies of the ALBA bloc and of Iran are atrophied and overly dependent upon extractive industries. There are no religious or cultural ties that connect them, nor are there linguistic or historic linkages. In fact, geography itself would seem to mitigate against any possible relationship.

The question, then, is why has this relationship manifested itself, and more specifically, what does Iran receive from ALBA? There are at least three areas in which Iran finds a foothold in the Americas, and a relationship with ALBA, to be useful.

Diplomatic

Iran has received significant diplomatic support from the ALBA bloc. ALBA members have repeatedly voted against sanctions on Iran at the United Nations, and have supported the Islamic Republic's resistance to oversight by that body's nuclear watchdog, the International Atomic Energy Agency (IAEA). Moreover, they provided former Iranian President Mahmoud Ahmadinejad and new President Hassan Rouhani with an opportunity to showcase Iran on the world stage as a legitimate nation that is not isolated internationally. Through this relationship, Iran has opened six new embassies (for a total of eleven) across the region and has started a Spanish language broadcast— *HispanTV*—that reaches out to millions in the Spanish-speaking world and provides a platform from which Iran can voice its rhetoric.

Economic/Trade

Iran and the nations of ALBA have signed a significant number of preferential trade deals. Exactly how many is unclear, but experts estimate the number to be in the hundreds over the past decade. These agreements are usually secret, and for this reason their implementation is difficult to follow. As one assessment has described:

> Iran and Venezuela are launching joint ventures in sectors such as energy, agriculture, manufacturing, housing, and infrastructure. In 2007, the two countries announced that they were finalizing a $2 billion joint-fund for their numerous projects, including those in Nicaragua, Bolivia, and other partner countries. Already a major investor in the $4 billion Ayacucho oil field joint project, Iran agreed in 2008 to invest an additional $760 million in Venezuela's energy sector. In 2009, Venezuela agreed to invest $760 million in Iran's South Pars gas field. In late October 2010, as collective sanctions on the Iranian economy started to bite, Venezuela offered an $800 million investment package in Iran's Pars Field gas sector. [10]

Many analysts believe that there are various methods for laundering Iran's sanctioned funds and injecting them into the Latin American financial system. This is particularly the case because ALBA's virtual currency, the SUCRE, could be used as an ideal sanctions-busting method for Iran to gain access to U.S. dollars. [11]

Criminal Activity

This final area of activity is probably the most extensive. Iran has reportedly used its relationship with ALBA to bolster the presence of its clerical army, the Revolutionary Guard Corps, in the hemisphere, and to cells affiliated with Lebanese Shi'a militia Hezbollah there. The purpose of this presence is twofold.

First, Hezbollah uses its increased presence in Latin America to fundraise for ongoing global operations. There are large Syrian/Lebanese diaspora communities in Latin America, especially in Venezuela, Argentina and Brazil. These are important sources of revenue and support for both Iran and Hezbollah. The Tri-Border Area at the intersection of Argentina, Brazil and Paraguay, and more recently Venezuela's Margarita Island, have served as a significant base of operations for Iranian and Iranian-linked militants thanks to its permissive environment and lax oversight.[12] Such a situation is replicated in miniature in many of the free trade zones that populate the Americas.[13]

Second, by recruiting, indoctrinating and proselytizing among Latin American citizens, Iran is enhancing its rapid response capability in the event of a military contingency or a political crisis—for example, if the United States or Israel strikes its nuclear facilities.[14] The past few years have witnessed several attempted Iranian-sponsored attacks that were organized and planned in Latin America. These include the thwarted attempt to assassinate the Saudi Ambassador in Washington, D.C.,[15] the cyber-hacking attempts by the Iranian ambassador in Mexico and the Venezuelan consul in Miami,[16] and the arrest of several alleged Iranian-connected terrorists in Mexico.[17]

The illicit activities necessary to fund, organize, train and equip a terrorist network of this magnitude are only possible because of the relatively permissive operating environment that exists within ALBA countries. Other terrorist groups active in the region, including the FARC, ETA, Shining Path and MRTA, all of whom operate with relative impunity within ALBA countries, have similarly exploited this environment. Under these conditions, Iran and Hezbollah have found ample opportunity to conduct illicit activities; for example, in the case of Hezbollah, by establishing an extensive drug running network that it now uses to fund its operations.[18] Much of this drug running is done through Venezuela, which has been criticized by the U.S. Department of State for its lack of cooperation and poor efforts in the fight against narcotics trafficking. According to investigator and regional security expert Douglas Farah:

> There is growing evidence of the merging of the Bolivarian Revolution's criminal/terrorist pipeline activities and those of the criminal-terrorist pipeline of radical Islamist groups (Hezbollah in particular) supported by the Iranian regime. The possibility opens a series of new security challenges for the Unit-

ed States and its allies in Latin America. The 1994 Hezbollah and Iranian
bombing of the AMIA building in Buenos Aires, Argentina, is a useful reminder that these groups can and do operate in Latin America.[19]

ALBA'S MOTIVATIONS

The interests of the ALBA countries lie in the same three general areas that
propel Iranian engagement in the Americas.

Diplomatic

Like Iran, the ALBA bloc is seeking a diplomatic and psychological victory
in its fight against the United States. By making common cause with the
world's most volatile geopolitical player, the bloc demonstrates its willingness to oppose the established international order. This is important, because
the political project of ALBA is not one based on representative republican
democracy, but rather the attempt to (re)create *nouveau* authoritarian regimes, which reject the principles of democracy that have become the norm
in the Western Hemisphere since the ratification of the Inter-American Democratic Charter.

Member states know that this will bring them into conflict with the United States, Canada, and other democracies in the region. At the same time,
however, the alliance with Iran serves to further polarize the region and shift
the perceived balance of power in Latin America in their favor.

Economic/Trade

Iran has shown that it is willing to lose a significant percentage of its investment in order to launder its money. The Islamic Republic therefore represents an injection of unrestricted funds that the small, relatively poor countries of ALBA can use for partisan political purposes. After all, the Bolivarian revolution is an expensive political project, because it rests upon the
assumption that legitimacy is purchased at the ballot box. This means that
candidates must spend an exorbitant amount of money to buy political pat-
ronage, manipulate electoral registries and ultimately continue to win elections that allow them to advance their authoritarian maneuvers.

Aside from winning elections, ALBA leaders rest their legitimacy on
funneling mass social spending toward sectors of society that provide them
with an uneven playing field. Doing so is expensive and risky, but so far has
paid dividends throughout the region. Not only are most of these governments viewed as legitimate by their respective populations, as well as the
international and regional order, but also they are occasionally applauded for
their ongoing electoral and political maneuvers. In this light, Iran is seen as

an "investor" and backer of ALBA's overall regional strategy. This benefit can turn even more important if Iran is able to convince Western powers to lift sanctions restricting its access to international markets.

Criminal Activity

Venezuela, Ecuador, and Bolivia have effectively become narco-states.[20] Led by Venezuela, ALBA sees the strengthening of the FARC as the only way to eventually bring the government of Colombia into the fold. Colombia was the jewel in the crown of Bolivar's *Gran Colombia*, and without it, this hemispheric project is not complete. Over the years, the FARC has become a transnational drug cartel, controlling cocaine production and transit from the Andes. ALBA nations realize that enabling a permissive environment for drug trafficking and money laundering in their respective countries will allow the FARC to have access to more resources and territory and thus continue its struggle for control of Colombia. Therefore, ALBA's leadership has been helping the FARC move from military to political relevance, as seen during the recent peace talks in Colombia. In fact, the ongoing peace talks now underway in Havana are the culmination of this strategy, providing the FARC the political path to continue to exist and make a transition to electoral politics—a game that ALBA already dominates in Latin America.

Naturally, Iran and its terrorist proxies overlap and interact illegally with these organized crime and drug networks. The FARC has pre-existing relationships with the aforementioned terrorist groups that predate the rise of ALBA, and the illicit infrastructure thereby created has since been expanded under the permissive environments of the ALBA governments. As much as Iranian investments are useful, the added benefit of illicit drug money from Hezbollah and the FARC provides even more much-needed currency to ALBA's expensive political projects.

Finally, under the tenets of asymmetric warfare, the ALBA governments view Iran as an experienced and battle-tested ally that can advise them on how to move their political project forward. Iran's paramilitary militias, such as the *Basij*, provide needed strategic and tactical know-how to improve ALBA's own militias. This was particularly relevant during the 2014 insecurity crisis in Venezuela, in which asymmetric actors, trained and armed by Cuban and Iranian advisors, savagely attacked protestors in a manner similar to how Iran quelled its own "Green Revolution" in 2009.[21]

A SINISTER SYNERGY

For all of these reasons, ALBA has become Iran's partner, and perhaps its strongest ally in the world. The shared interests that animate this mutually beneficial relationship only serve to complement the one thing that these disparate countries have in common—a mutual revolution that will bring about what Iran's ayatollahs, Chávez, and Castro have all called a "New World Order."

After the death of Hugo Chávez on March 5, 2013, many said that Iran had lost its best regional ally. Nevertheless, Chávez's successor, Nicolas Maduro (previously, president of the ALBA bank and Venezuela's former Foreign Minister, tasked with ALBA's implementation) has continued to carry forward the Bolivarian project. The re-election of Rafael Correa in Ecuador and Daniel Ortega in Nicaragua has further solidified the idea that the ALBA project will continue its established trajectory. So has the recent re-election of Juan Manuel Santos in Colombia, who appears determined to offer the FARC the legitimacy it needs to transform into a political party.

As an observer member of the bloc, Iran will certainly continue to use this alliance to increase its foothold in the region. ALBA, meanwhile, will continue to rely on Iran as its most strategic partner outside of Latin America. To hammer home this point, ALBA's former executive secretary, Amenhotep Zambrano, was recently appointed as the new Venezuelan Ambassador in Tehran.

While it is unclear what would happen should Iran obtain a nuclear weapon, or should Hezbollah be successful in carrying out another attack in the Americas, it is clear that the Iran/ALBA axis represents Washington's greatest challenge in the Hemisphere.

NOTES

1. Joel Hirst, *The ALBA: Inside Venezuela's Bolivarian Alliance* (CreateSpace Independent Publishing Platform, 2012).

2. Stephen Johnson, *Iran's Influence in the Americas* (Washington, D.C.: Center for Strategic and International Studies, February 2012).

3. "Declaracion Conjunta entre el Presidente de la Republica Bolivariana de Venezuela y el Presidente del Consejo de Estado de la Republica de Cuba para la creación del ALBA," December 14, 2004, http://www.cuba.cu/gobierno/discursos/2004/esp/d141204e.html (accessed 2013).

4. Centro de Investigaciones Economicas, *Gasto Publico Anunciado por el Gobierno de Venezuela*, 2005–2010.

5. Joseph Humire, *Testimony before the House Homeland Security Committee Subcommittee on Oversight and Management Efficiency*, July 9, 2013, http://docs.house.gov/meetings/HM/HM09/20130709/101046/HHRG-113-HM09-Wstate-HumireJ-20130709-U1.pdf (accessed 2013).

6. Jo Becker, "Beirut Bank Seen as a Hub of Hezbollah's Financing," The New York Times, Dec. 13, 2011, http://www.nytimes.com/2011/12/14/world/middleeast/beirut-bank-seen-as-a-hub-of-hezbollahs-financing.html?pagewanted=all&_r=1&.

7. United Nations Office on Drugs and Crime, *World Drug Report* 2012, http://www.unodc.org/documents/data-and-analysis/WDR2012/WDR_2012_web_small.pdf (accessed 2013).

8. Roger Noriega, *Testimony before the U.S. House of Representatives Committee on Foreign Relations Subcommittee on Terrorism and Nonproliferation*, March 13, 2013.

9. Author's interviews, Miami, Florida, April 2012.

10. Richard Javad Heydarian, "Iran's Adventures in Latin America," *Foreign Policy in Focus* 2010, http://www.fpif.org/articles/irans_adventures_in_latin_america (accessed 2013).

11. Mercedes Alvadro and Jeffrey T. Lewis, "Who Needs Bitcoin? Venezuela Has Its 'Sucre,'" *Wall Street Journal*, January 2, 2014, http://online.wsj.com/news/articles/SB10001424052702304202204579256062854362716 (accessed 2014).

12. John Barnam, "Hezbollah's Latin American Home," *Security Management* 2013, http://www.securitymanagement.com/article/hezbollahs-latin-american-home (accessed 2014).

13. Adam Kredo, "Kirchner Opens Door to Latin America for Iran," *The Washington Free Beacon,* July 9, 2013, http://freebeacon.com/national-security/kirchner-opens-door-to-latin-america-for-iran/ (accessed 2013).

14. John Miller, "Ex Revolutionary Guard Member: Iran Ready with Terror Plans to Hit U.S. If Israel Attacks," *CBS,* July 19, 2012, http://www.cbsnews.com/8301-505263_162-57475439/ex-revolutionary-guard-member-iran-ready-with-terror-plans-to-hit-u.s-if-israel-attacks/ (accessed 2013).

15. Evan Perez, "U.S. Accuses Iran in Plot," *Wall Street Journal,* October 12, 2011, http://online.wsj.com/article/AP930269703c444cffa8b3509649f3c926.html (accessed 2013).

16. Chris Irvine and Damien McElroy, "U.S. Expels Venezuela Consul General amid Cyber Plot Allegations," *Telegraph* (London), January 8, 2012, http://www.telegraph.co.uk/news/worldnews/southamerica/venezuela/9001240/US-expels-Venezuela-consul-general-amid-cyber-attack-plot-allegations.html (accessed 2013).

17. "Hezbollah Suspected Terrorist Arrested in Merida," *The Yucatan Times*, September 10, 2012, http://www.theyucatantimes.com/2012/09/hezbollah-suspected-terrorist-arrested-in-merida/ (accessed 2013).

18. Matthew Levitt, "Hizbullah Narco-Terrorism: A Growing Cross-Border Threat," *IHS Defense, Risk, and Security*, September 2012, http://www.washingtoninstitute.org/uploads/Levitt20120900_1.pdf (accessed 2013).

19. Douglas Farah, *Testimony before the Senate Foreign Relations Committee Subcommittee on Western Hemisphere, Peace Corps, and Global Narcotics Affairs*, February 16, 2012, http://www.strategycenter.net/docLib/20120218_Testimony_Farah_IranLA_021612.pdf (accessed 2013).

20. International Institute for Strategic Studies, "FARC Files: Venezuela, Ecuador and the Secret Archive of Raul Reyes," May 10, 2011.

21. Joseph Humire, "Iran Props up Venezuela's Militias," *Washington Times*, 2014, http://www.washingtontimes.com/news/2014/mar/17/humire-irans-basij-props-up-venezuelas-repressive-/?page=all (accessed 2014).

Chapter Four

The Southern Cone

Iran's Backdoor

Iván Witker

At first glance, a region originally colonized by Spain and Portugal in the Catholic-European tradition seems an incongruous "bridge" into the Western Hemisphere for the Islamic Republic of Iran. Nevertheless, many Iranian leaders see Latin America as another chapter in a global anti-imperialist, anti-Western, and anti-Zionist revolution.

Since at least the turn of the century, Iranian doctrine toward Latin America has included the idea of "land of mission," meaning that all work should be done in cooperation with local political partners. In recent years, Iran's political partners in Latin America have become more diversified. Not only does the Islamic Republic maintain its traditional association with Venezuela and Cuba, it has also moved aggressively to expand further south, through the Andes, into the Southern Cone.

Following the death of Hugo Chávez, and in the wake of increasing instability in Venezuela, Iran understands that it can potentially lose Caracas as its regional gateway. As a result, the ayatollahs have begun strategically expanding Iran's footprint in the region, so that a post-Chávez era does not disrupt their ambitions in Latin America. Bolivia has quickly become a major ally in this regard, and could potentially displace Venezuela as the partner of choice for the Islamic Republic. Indeed, recent developments between Tehran and La Paz suggest that this may already be occurring. The surrounding Southern Cone region therefore represents an important component of Iran's strategic designs in Latin America.

ANOTHER BATTLEFIELD FOR IRAN

The Southern Cone is a geographic sub-region composed of the southern-most areas of South America below the Tropic of Capricorn. It typically is defined as consisting of Chile, Argentina, Paraguay and Uruguay, and even parts of southeastern Brazil. Among the primary interests and objectives for Iran in this geographic area are:

- *Political and ideological influence,* since Argentina and Brazil contain the largest Muslim populations in the region.
- *Increased commerce and trade,* since Argentina, Brazil and Uruguay are Iran's largest trade partners in the region.
- *A search for strategic materials,* such as uranium, thorium, tantalum and lithium, deposits of which are evident in southeastern Brazil, western Bolivia, and parts of Chile and Peru.
- *Logistical and asymmetric connections* within the historic Tri-Border Area (TBA) of Argentina, Paraguay, and Brazil and to the new TBA between Chile, Bolivia, and Peru.
- *The acquisition of a larger geographic area of influence* that can be connected to the ALBA nations.

Iran is pursuing these objectives throughout the Southern Cone, and doing so in various ways.

Chile

Formal relations between Iran and Chile have diminished since the 1994 AMIA attack in neighboring Argentina. Chile currently has no embassy in Tehran, and the Chilean government has not afforded much opportunity for dialogue or interaction with the Islamic Republic outside of traditional day-to-day bilateral diplomacy. However, Chile merits special attention because its foreign policy has left it vulnerable to Iranian intelligence operations in the region. Its close proximity to Bolivia is also of concern, given the lax border controls between the two countries.

Bolivia is landlocked, and thus needs access to seaports. The Free Trade Zones of Iquique, Arica and other seaports in the northern part of Chile therefore represent inviting targets. Chilean authorities keep a watchful eye on Islamist activities in these zones, because they have been used in the past as transit points for drugs, funds, and other illicit products on behalf of the Lebanese terrorist group Hezbollah.[1] The coastal ports of these cities provide neighboring Bolivia with a shipping route for moving material to and from Iran.

For instance, on August 28, 2012, Brazilian and Bolivian authorities found two tons of tantalite in garbage bags in the office garage of the Venezuelan military attaché in La Paz. This strategic mineral, which has dual-use military applications when refined, was reportedly mined out of Guajará-Mirim in Brazil and transported via smuggling routes through Bolivia to Arica, Chile, where it was allegedly destined for transport by boat to Venezuela and then on to Iran.[2]

The arrival of ships from the Islamic Republic of Iran Shipping Lines (IRISL) to Chilean seaports is also disturbing, given that the Iranian shipping conglomerate is currently under sanctions for its role in Iran's nuclear and military programs. In 2009, two Iranian ships, the *MV Filbert* and the *MV Vobster*, sailed under foreign flags as a way to gain access to Chilean seaports in Ventanas and Huasco. This reflagging scheme happened again in 2010 in the ports of Tocopilla, Guayacan, and Valparaiso.[3] To casual observers, the presence of these ships may not constitute a significant threat; however, their activity is suspicious, given that the volume of commercial trade between the two nations is relatively small.

While Iran has expressed interest in a variety of Chilean industries, this has amounted solely to sporadic exchanges of copper and oil.[4] Many of the planned large-scale joint commercial projects have not come to fruition, due to Iran's reluctance to move forward on what are considered high-risk ventures.

Trade between the two nations is negligible, as are cultural exchanges. Yet this lack of economic and diplomatic activity does not mean Chile is tangential to Iran's strategic agenda in Latin America. Formal efforts by the Iranian government may have not produced significant commercial and cultural ties, however, its informal network in the country is quite substantial, as evidenced by the incremental increase in the number of Chilean converts to Shi'a Islam.[5] In Chile's case, many of these conversions can be attributed to the *Centro Cultural Islamico de Las Condes* in the capital, Santiago, as well as to smaller mosques and cultural centers in Iquique, Viña del Mar and Puerto Montt. These Islamic centers have strong connections to other Iranian efforts in the Southern Cone, namely in Argentina.

Argentina

Argentina's relationship with Iran is one of its most long-standing in the region, dating back to 1902. However, ties took a turn for the worse in the 1990s, when the Islamic Republic facilitated two bombings on Israeli/Jewish targets in Buenos Aires. There is little doubt (both within Argentina and globally) that the Iranian government played a decisive role in these attacks, particularly in the 1994 bombing of the AMIA Jewish center. Argentine authorities have accused seven Iranian officials and one Lebanese militant (now deceased) in the attack, but no one has yet been formally charged. The most notorious of these suspects is Iranian cleric Mohsen Rabbani, who is known to have indoctrinated multiple disciples in Argentina. Rabbani trained these disciples to use Islamic charities in the country as backdoor channels to the Islamic Republic, and to insinuate themselves into the activities of the Argentine government.

The two most prominent Rabbani disciples active in Argentina (and neighboring countries) are Edgardo Ruben "Suhail" Assad and his brother-in-law Santiago Paz Bullrich, who goes by his Islamic name Abdul Karim Paz.[6] Together these activists serve as Iran's "informal ambassadors" in Latin America and travel throughout the region unifying and radicalizing Islamic communities.[7] In particular, Suhail Assad is a well-known figure in Chilean Islamic circles, having received his bachelor's degree in philosophy from the *Adolfo Ibañez* University in Santiago.[8] Moreover, Assad is a guest lecturer at many prominent universities, including the *Universidad de Santiago* and the *Pontificia Universidad Católica de Chile*.

Assad and Karim Paz both began their tutelage under Rabbani in the 1980s, working at the At-Tahuid mosque that had been founded by Rabbani in 1983. This prominent mosque, located in Buenos Aires, continues to serve as a hub for Islamic leaders throughout the region. Sympathetic socialist activists, such as Argentina's former undersecretary for Land and Social Habitat, Luis D'Elia, are also frequent guests there. D'Elia has been suspected by Argentine authorities of receiving financial support from the Islamic Republic, and has taken several trips to Iran.[9] In one of these trips, D'Elia took the opportunity to visit Qom and record a controversial interview with Mohsen Rabbani.

Today, there are several Islamic organizations in Argentina linked to Rabbani's extensive regional network. The work of these groups and their respective activists was influential in prompting Argentina's recent reconsideration of its political posture toward Iran—a rethink that culminated in the controversial "truth" commission initiated in 2013 by Argentine Foreign Minister Hector Timerman. The commission was set to re-investigate the AMIA attacks, but was later annulled by an Argentine federal court. As of this writing, the Fernández de Kirchner regime is appealing the verdict. Even absent the commission, however, Argentina remains important to Iran as an intellectual hub to promote its image and ideas in neighboring countries, particularly Paraguay, Uruguay, and Bolivia.

Paraguay

Iran enjoyed a burgeoning relationship with Paraguay during the tenure of its former president, Fernando Armindo "Lugo" Méndez (2008–2012). Unfortunately for Iran, Lugo's term was short-lived; he was impeached and removed from office by the Paraguayan congress in 2012 over a controversial land purchase that led to the death of a handful of police and close to a dozen farmers.[10]

Iran's proximity to Lugo was partially attributed to the support the politician received for his presidential campaign from Venezuela, as well as from the sizeable Islamic population in Ciudad del Este. This bred a sympathetic attitude in Asunción upon Lugo's election, with former foreign minister Hector Lactognata expressing an interest in expanding relations, and reiterated his support for Iran's resistance to imperialism. Iran's former deputy foreign minister later visited Paraguay in 2011 to begin work on several documents relating to bilateral cooperation, hoping this would bring about a major advancement of Iran-Paraguay relations.[11]

Yet despite this display of solidarity, there is no evidence of an increase in the size of the Iranian mission in Paraguay. Nor is there evidence to suggest a decrease in the clandestine activities of Iranian terror proxy Hezbollah in Ciudad del Este, within the Tri-Border Area, along the Paraná River. Hezbollah is known to use the TBA to smuggle material, money, and other illicit products throughout the Southern Cone. In 2002, the arrest of Asad Barakat, a co-owner of one of the largest malls in Ciudad del Este and a known Hezbollah financier, unearthed a financial and smuggling network that stretched from Foz da Iquazco, Brazil through Paraguay into Iquique and Arica, Chile.[12]

Incidents like the Barakat case shed light on a concerning and persistent lack of anti-terrorism legislation, both in Paraguay and throughout much of the rest of Latin America. The Paraguayan government has professed ongoing vigilance in this regard, yet new president Horacio Cartes, a former businessman, holds a spotty record (having been investigated by the U.S. Drug Enforcement Agency in connection with several instances of money-laundering and illicit tobacco smuggling). This suggests that the Islamic Republic will, at the very least, be free to maintain its clandestine presence in the TBA in the years ahead.

Uruguay

On the surface, Uruguay's relations with Iran revolve around commercial activity, particularly the export of rice to the Islamic Republic through the port of Concepción. When Iran stopped buying rice from Argentina in the 1990s (a byproduct of the AMIA investigation), Uruguay became its new principal supplier of the foodstuff. In 2012, Uruguay additionally entered into discussions regarding a food-for-oil exchange with Iran, an arrangement common to other nations in the Southern Cone. While these talks have not yet borne fruit, many believe Uruguay is motivated to pursue this kind of exchange by a desire to avoid the dollar.[13]

The commercial relationship between Uruguay and Iran nearly took a turn for the worse in July 2011, when Iran's former ambassador to Uruguay, Hojatollah Soltani, denied the Jewish Holocaust while speaking at a cultural event in Montevideo. Needless to say, these comments were not well received by prominent Jewish circles in Uruguay. Uruguay's government was quick to do damage control, however; while condemning Soltani's statements, Foreign Minister Luis Almagro also made clear that diplomatic and trade relations would not be affected by the incident. [14]

This was clear a year later, when Uruguay's national airline, PLUNA, went bankrupt and its CEO invited more than 20 Iranian "businessmen" to discuss a buyout deal. [15] As a result of significant pressure from the country's Jewish community, the deal was put on hold. Nevertheless, the exchange revealed a close relationship between the Islamic Republic and the administration of José Alberto Pepe Mújica—one that continues to this day.

Bolivia

Partnership with the aforementioned countries of the Southern Cone would represent a strategic advantage for Iran, but none are more significant to the Islamic Republic than is Bolivia. Bolivia has the potential to serve as both a base of operations for the Islamic Republic in the region and a vehicle by which to expand its influence throughout South America. And, in contrast to the countries mentioned above, the partnership between La Paz and Tehran is growing by leaps and bounds.

In recent years, several significant treaties have been signed between Iran and Bolivia. Particularly noteworthy is a June 2012 anti-narco trafficking accord, which explicitly states that Iran will provide training and advice on anti-narcotics operations to the Bolivian police and army, while also providing equipment and training for technical and support staff. [16] The agreement establishes a framework and a pretext for an Iranian military presence in the region. It is all the more significant because it stands in stark contrast with Bolivia's counter-narcotics relationship with America; in 2008, Bolivian president Evo Morales expelled the U.S. Drug Enforcement Administration (DEA) and cut off all cooperation on narco-trafficking, a move that resulted in an explosion in the production of coca throughout the country. As such, the joint Bolivian-Iranian agreement appears to simply be a pretext for closer military and paramilitary cooperation, and for an expanded Iranian strategic presence in Bolivia.

Strategic resources factor into the bilateral relationship as well. Bolivia is one of the most resource-rich countries in the region, and has the potential to further the Islamic Republic's quest for strategic resources for its missile and nuclear programs. Indeed, some believe Bolivia has provided the Iranian regime with uranium ore. [17] And while many of the political and economic promises made by Iran to Bolivia have not materialized, officials in La Paz do not appear deterred from pursuing a stronger relationship with Tehran.

AN EMERGING THREAT

Iran's growing influence in Latin America's Southern Cone has taken many forms. However, the common denominator of this outreach has been the underlying anti-imperialist, anti-American, and anti-Zionist sentiments, as well as radical religious ideas that are being spread as a result.

These ideas take root in Argentina and continually spread up north, making the Southern Cone a source of intellectual ammunition for Iran's ambitions in Latin America. But ideas are not all that is being spread. An increasingly important base of operations in Bolivia, within the heart of South America, serves as an axis point for Iran's pursuit of strategic raw materials that are prevalent throughout the region. This can potentially facilitate an even greater Iranian presence than currently exists, as Iran exploits a new stateless Tri-Border Area (TBA) between northern Chile (Arica and Iquique), southern Peru (Tacna and Puno), and Bolivia (from El Alto to the Iranian embassy in La Paz).

A sizeable region full of porous borders, this pacific TBA provides the high concentration of Iranian agents in landlocked Bolivia with several clandestine routes that pass through seaports in Chile. A sleeping giant in the broader regional anti-terrorism effort, Chile is increasingly serving as a zone of entry/exit for Iranian agents to move undetected in the region. The northern part of the country has a historic criminal-terrorist pipeline that extends through the Southern Cone, into Paraguay where Iran enjoys a logistical network that extends into southeastern Brazil. Uruguay connects this network back to Argentina, coming full circle and providing Iran with a larger geographic area of influence. Moving money, drugs, and agents of influence, Iran's presence and activities in the Southern Cone have all the makings of an emerging threat to further destabilize the region.

NOTES

1. Marc Perelman, "Feds Call Chile Resort a Terror Hot Spot," *Forward*, January 3, 2003, http://forward.com/articles/9036/feds-call-chile-resort-a-terror-hot-spot/.

2. German Rojas, "Tantalita hallada en La Paz fue extraida en Brasil y tenia como destino Iran," Eju.tv (La Paz), September 21, 2012, http://eju.tv/2012/09/tantalita-hallada-en-la-paz-fue-extrada-en-brasil-y-tena-como-destino-irn/.

3. Author interviews with port authorities in northern Chile, as part of a research project to assess threat vulnerabilities to Chile's northern coast, June 2012.

4. See Stephen Johnson, *Iran's Influence in the Americas* (Washington, D.C.: Center for Strategic and International Studies, March 2012), 34, http://csis.org/files/publication/120312__Johnson_Iran'sInfluence_web.pdf.

5. The first wave of Muslim immigrants to Chile began in the nineteenth century, but by the 1980s a sizeable Islamic population had settled in the country. This population consists primarily of Syrian, Lebanese and Palestinian immigrants. See http://islamicpostonline.com/article/islam_alive_and_well_chile for more discussion on Islam in Chile.

6. Abdul Karim Paz is an Argentine convert to Islam, who belongs to a prominent family in Buenos Aires. He worked alongside his mentor Mohsen Rabbani at the At-Tahuid Mosque for several years leading up to the AMIA attacks. Managing many of Rabbani's influence operations aimed at the Islamic community in Argentina, Karim Paz was influential in developing the younger generation of radical Islamists in Argentina, including Suhail Assad. After the AMIA attacks, Karim Paz escaped Argentina with Rabbani and studied in Qom for five years, only to return to Argentina in the late 1990s to take over where Rabbani left off. Karim Paz is currently affiliated with several Islamic cultural centers in Chile and Bolivia, and succeeded Rabbani at the At-Tahuid Mosque in Buenos Aires.

7. Joseph Humire, "Iran's Informal Ambassadors in Latin America," *Fox News Latino*, February 18, 2012, http://latino.foxnews.com/latino/politics/2012/02/18/joseph-humire-irans-informal-ambassadors-to-latin-america/.

8. Born in Argentina and of Lebanese decent, Suhail Assad moved to Lebanon in his twenties to study Islamic studies and later received a Ph.D. in Islamic theology from the Al Mustafa Open University in Beirut. He also studied Islamic Culture and Civilization extensively in Qom, Iran under the tutelage of Rabbani. Fluent in Spanish, Farsi, Arabic and English, Assad is an important asset for Iran in Latin America and currently directs the Center for Iranian-Latin American Cultural Exchange based in Caracas, Venezuela. Splitting his time traveling back and forth to Qom, Iran, Assad is the primary instructor for Latin American students visiting the Islamic Republic.

9. In a meeting of the Hebrew society in Pilar, Argentina, Federal Judge Daniel Rafecas said: "I'm convinced that the Iranian embassy is financing with a lot money many groups and Mr. D'Elia is not from this." As cited in *Clarin* (Buenos Aires), April 1, 2011, http://www.atfa.org/delia-once-again-in-a-controversy-over-his-ties-to-teheran/.

10. For more, see "Paraguay's President Fernando Lugo Ousted from Office," Associated Press, June 22, 2012, http://www.theguardian.com/world/2012/jun/22/paraguay-fernando-lugo-ousted .

11. Anna Mahjar-Barducci, "Iran in Brazil, Paraguay and Uruguay," Gatestone Institute, August 24, 2011, http://www.gatestoneinstitute.org/2372/iran-brazil-paraguay-uruguay.

12. Blanca Madani, "Hezbollah's Global Finance Network: The Triple Frontier," *Middle East Intelligence Bulletin* 4, no. 1, January 2002, http://www.meforum.org/meib/articles/0201_l2.htm.

13. Ibid.; Johnson, *Iran's Influence in the Americas*, 39.

14. Anna Mahjar-Barducci, "Uruguay's Diplomacy with Iran," Gatestone Institute, August 19, 2011, http://www.gatestoneinstitute.org/2365/uruguay-iran-holocaust-denial.

15. "Vidalín acerca otro uruguayo para Pluna; viene de Irán," Republica.com.uy (Montevideo), November 3, 2012, http://www.republica.com.uy/empresario-interesado-en-pluna/.

16. "Iran Will Train Anti-Narcotics Force in Bolivia," *El Nuevo Herald*, June 20, 2012, http://www.elnuevoherald.com/2012/06/19/1232800/iran-adiestrara-a-la-fuerza-antidroga.html.

17. "Secret Document: Venezuela, Bolivia Supplying Iran with Uranium," Associated Press, May 25, 2009, http://www.haaretz.com/news/secret-document-venezuela-bolivia-supplying-iran-with-uranium-1.276675.

Chapter Five

Iran and Islamic Extremism in Brazil

Leonardo Coutinho

The first clear indication of the presence of Lebanon's radical Shi'ite militia, Hezbollah, in Latin America was a car bomb that exploded at 2:42 pm on March 17, 1992, in front of the Israeli Embassy in Buenos Aires, the capital of Argentina. Hezbollah immediately identified the attack as an act of retaliation for the death of its leader, Abbas al-Musawi, just one month prior, during an Israeli military offensive.[1] Twenty-nine people were killed during the attack in Buenos Aires, and 242 more were injured.

Nearly two years later, a second explosion struck the Argentine Jewish Mutual Association (AMIA) building, killing 85 people and injuring over 300.[2] Once again, authorities suspected that Hezbollah had been the perpetrator. But this time, they believed, the group had acted with the support of Iran, its principal state sponsor and progenitor.[3] Investigators in Argentina asserted that the attack had been planned by Iran's government and executed by Hezbollah cells active in South America. Moreover, according to the prosecutors involved in the case, the bombing had likely been planned at the Iranian Embassy in Buenos Aires—and Mohsen Rabbani, the Iranian cultural attaché in Buenos Aires at the time, is believed to have been one of the principal organizers.[4]

A connection to Brazil was also uncovered. Prosecutors discovered that one of the suspect's mobile phones was purchased in the Brazilian city of Foz do Iguaçu, located in the Tri-Border Area where Argentina, Brazil and Paraguay intersect. Moreover, additional evidence suggested that Brazil might have been used as a base for the preparation of the attacks. Samuel Salman el-Reda, a Colombian of Lebanese origin, was charged with serving as the logistics coordinator for both bombings. El-Reda owned a house in Foz do Iguaçu, where he lived until the time of the AMIA bombing, following which he fled to Lebanon.[5]

A THRIVING CLANDESTINE NETWORK

Some two decades after these bombings, the perpetrators have never been brought to justice. However, in April 2011, Brazil's weekly *Veja* newsmagazine published an exposé detailing that one of the suspects had facilitated several of Mohsen Rabbani's secret visits to South America (and specifically to Brazil).[6] In addition, according to supporting documents, the Brazilian police not only knew of Rabbani's presence but also attempted to arrest him; the mission, however, was aborted for undisclosed reasons. Sources close to the Brazilian government claimed that Rabbani entered Brazil via Venezuela, using official documents but traveling under a false identity.[7] Utilizing the regular flights between Tehran and Caracas operated by the Venezuelan state-owned airline *Conviasa*, Rabbani—despite being the subject of an active arrest warrant issued by the International Criminal Police Organization (INTERPOL) for his role in the AMIA attack—was able to travel repeatedly to Brazil. In September 2010, for example, he is known to have stayed with his brother, Mohammad Bagher Rabbani, in Curitiba, the capital of Brazil's southern Paraná state. In 2009 and 2011, Mohammad Bagher Rabbani applied to renew his visa to stay in Brazil. The Ministry of Justice granted his first request, but denied the second—likely because of information regarding his role in aiding the travel and lodging of his brother, a suspected terrorist.[8]

Mohammed Bagher Rabbani's role, however, goes further. Brazilian intelligence agencies are aware that he acted as his brother's "ambassador" in Brazil. As revealed in the April 2011 *Veja* exposé, during his time in Curitiba, Mohammed Bagher Rabbani controlled the funding of Islamic centers and the recruitment of young Brazilians who were then sent to the Iranian city of Qom for "Islamic studies."[9] Another article by the same magazine, titled "Terror Professor," details this role:

> The Federal Police and ABIN, the country's secret service agency, have followed Rabbani's recruitment of Brazilians for courses abroad for the last four years. Rabbani himself, with the help of trusted associates, chooses who will travel. Since 2007, three groups of Brazilians have visited Iran. There are plenty of reasons for such official surveillance. The course has strong religious content, but this is not the main reason for concern. Rather, students of one of Rabbani's classes have confided that during the trips they visited the facilities of the radical Lebanese group Hezbollah, considered a terror organization by many countries, including the United States. Reports to which *Veja* had access indicate that professor Rabbani's courses are a gateway to terrorism. According to these documents, classes are used for preaching radicalism and include training in military camps.[10]

One of the most noteworthy of Bagher Rabbani's recruits in Brazil is Rodrigo Jalloul.[11] Less than thirty years old, Jalloul is one of the younger

Islamic leaders in Brazil, and is the first to reach the title of *sheikh* as a result of taking various courses and being indoctrinated in Qom, Iran. The grandson of Lebanese and Spanish immigrants, Jalloul grew up in an Islamic neighborhood in São Paulo, selling contraband in commercial centers managed and run by the Lebanese Diaspora. Jalloul began attending a local mosque in the Brás neighborhood of São Paulo at 18 years old. After three years of studying Islamic theology in Brazil, a local businessman, Abdallah Hammoud, invited Jalloul to study in Qom, Iran.

Following his indoctrination, Jalloul became the first Brazilian *sheikh* in Qom, and an assistant to Rabbani's efforts to increase Iran's outreach to this important South American country. Jalloul assumed an operational role in Brazil in order to minimize the risk of Mohsen Rabbani or his brother being arrested. Jalloul maintains an extensive network of connections throughout Latin America with former Qom disciples. [12]

In November of 2013, however, Jalloul was denied entry to Iran when he attempted to disembark at the airport in Tehran. He has refused to talk about his denial of entry into the Islamic Republic, but has continued to work at the local mosque in São Paulo. [13] Iran's refusal to allow entry to one of its Brazilian converts may indicate a change in strategy, one in which they will not necessarily give up on a subversive asset in what is considered a strategic country, but will simply be more cautious.

The existence of Islamist terrorist cells in Brazil, to date, is confirmed by copious official documents. For example, in 2009, the Brazilian Federal Police arrested a Lebanese man, Khaled Hussein Ali, for suspected involvement with al-Qaeda. [14] But despite extensive documentation linking Ali to terror activities, he was never indicted. This was in large part because Brazil has so far not codified any law that criminalizes terrorism. Furthermore, despite the fact that the police closely monitor the activity of extremist groups, Brazilian authorities vehemently deny that their country serves as an operational base for Islamist radicals. At least some officials, however, have admitted the presence—indeed, the prevalence—of Islamic radicalism in Brazil. [15] By way of confirmation, the U.S. Treasury Department has designated several individuals residing in Brazil as financiers of terrorist activities. [16]

In keeping with this assessment, ongoing investigations by Brazilian intelligence agencies in recent years have noted that Hezbollah cells operate within the country, and that these cells serve as an important source of revenue to fund the activities of the group. Currently, with Iran's economic assistance to Hezbollah diminished as a result of both Western sanctions and the ongoing civil war in Syria (which the Iranian regime is supporting extensively), the organization's activities linked to smuggling (cigarettes, narcotics, arms, and even counterfeit merchandise) have taken on greater importance.

RELATIONS ON THE UPSWING

Ties between Brazil and Iran date back to early cultural contacts at the turn of
the last century. However, it was not until 1961 when Brazil's diplomatic
representation in Tehran was elevated to the level of an Embassy. Later, in
1965, Shah Reza Pahlavi paid his first official visit to Brazil. From there, ties
began to strengthen through greater cultural contacts on the part of both
countries, which were manifested in the mutual dissemination of books and
films.

After the 1979 Revolution, however, relations declined, in large part be-
cause of Brazil's tilt toward Iran's regional rival, the regime of Saddam
Hussein in Iraq. During the subsequent Iran-Iraq war (1980–1988), the Bra-
zilian government was a major supplier of military equipment to the Iraqi
armed forces. Moreover, large Brazilian companies established branches in
Iraq to work on rebuilding its infrastructure. Brazil's rapprochement with
Iran took place only after the war and the end of military rule in Brazil.
Beginning in 1988, bilateral trade increased, weighted heavily toward the
Iranian importation of Brazilian products. Some of this commerce was military in nature; after eight years of exclusive sales to Saddam Hussein's re-
gime, Brazil began to offer EMB-312 *Tucano* aircraft to the Islamic Repub-
lic. For a number of years thereafter, Brazil also trained members of the
Iranian military to pilot the planes. [17]

The activities of Iranian-sponsored terrorist groups on Brazilian soil date
back to this period. The most prominent is Lebanese Hezbollah, which established itself in the Tri-border Area in the mid-to-late 1980s, with Iran's
assistance. Thereafter, a number of other radical Islamic organizations, both
Shi'a and Sunni, followed suit. Brazil continues to be used as an operational
and financial base by these organizations.

This infiltration has been facilitated, at least in part, by the notable im-
provement in relations that has taken place between Iran and Brazil over the
past decade. The rise to power of leftist President Luiz Inácio "Lula" da Silva
in January 2003 was a decisive moment for the evolution of bilateral relations. With President Lula's inauguration, "South-South alignment" became
a governmental priority—as did the Brazilian government's efforts to distance itself from the United States. In lieu of ties with Washington, Lula's
administration focused on international "underprivileged" partners as allies,
courting them for, among other things, support in Brazil's campaign for a
seat on the UN Security Council.

Notably, while Brazil took on a central role in these alliances, it also drew
criticism from many corners—including Brazilian diplomatic circles—for its
strategic choices. Many observers cautioned that a covenant between Brazil
and Iran, even if purely political, would lump the Latin American country
into a dangerous group of nations, which are the targets of global mistrust—

and that this strategy could even compromise Brazil's objectives at the United Nations.[18] The advice would later prove prescient.

Iran, meanwhile, found that its warming relations with Brazil helped facilitate a growing presence in Latin America. Iran's regional strategy focused in large part on countries with anti-American governments (such as Venezuela, Bolivia, and Ecuador), with whom it established a series of cultural, commercial and energy agreements. Relations with Brazil followed the same trajectory. In 2003, Brazilian state oil company *Petrobras* received permission to explore Iranian oil fields. The following year, the two countries signed a deal to facilitate commercial transactions. More agreements followed; in 2009 alone, three other international agreements were signed in the areas of trade, science and technology, arts, and energy production. Brazil also became a technology provider for Iran's construction of hydroelectric plants during this period.

Then, in 2010, Brazil and Iran signed a memorandum codifying a technical partnership for the exploration, extraction, and processing of minerals in Brazil.[19] Significantly, the agreement contained a troubling confidentiality clause:

> The Parties agree to maintain the confidentiality of documents, information and data. The Parties shall take all necessary measures in order to ensure that confidential matters will not be disclosed to third parts for any reason, without the prior written consent of the other Party. This confidentiality agreement applies to information and data generated from the date of signing of this Memorandum of Understanding.[20]

The clause, and the secrecy it provides, was clearly intended to safeguard strategic information exchanged between the two states. But the requirement was out of character with the transparency Brazil usually brings to its commercial ventures. Adding suspicion was the presumed military dimension of Iran's nuclear program, which fueled speculation that the memorandum could serve as a vehicle for furthering Iran's nuclear effort. These fears were fanned further by disclosures regarding Iran's mining activities in Venezuela and Bolivia, where the Islamic Republic was believed to be extracting uranium ore and other strategic minerals for use in its nuclear program.[21]

BACKWARD FROM LULA

The trajectory of ties between Iran and Brazil under the Lula government was unmistakably one of expansion. However, in January 2011, the bilateral relationship experienced a setback with the election of Dilma Rousseff to the Brazilian presidency. From early on in her tenure, Rousseff chose to publicly distance herself from Iran, both to shed the stigma of being a "stand-in" for

Lula while he waited out a term to run for the presidency again, and to show seriousness to the outside world as one of the storied "BRIC" countries (Brazil, Russia, India, and China).

In her first year in office, Rousseff made clear that her government would not tolerate irregularities in the name of unconditional partnership, as her predecessor had done. Moreover, the new Brazilian president, herself considered a human rights activist, looked unfavorably upon the Islamic Republic's track record in that sphere, and therefore supported the UN's establishment of a Special Rapporteur for Human Rights in Iran to investigate the conduct of the Iranian regime.

This change in attitude caused significant discomfort in Tehran, and led to protests by high-ranking Iranian officials. For instance, Behrouz Kamalvandi, the Iranian Deputy Foreign Minister for the Americas, attributed Brazil's turnaround to pressure from the United States. "The change in the Brazilian vote after the visit (of U.S. President Barack Obama), while the human rights situation in Iran has had no significant changes, compared with the previous meeting, is not a desirable sign for public opinion neither in Iran nor in Brazil," Kamalvandi charged.[22] Other Iranian officials took a similar stance. Ali Akbar Javanfekr, the spokesman for then-Iranian president Mahmoud Ahmadinejad, criticized the Brazilian government, and blamed Rousseff for having "destroyed" years of good relations Iran had built up with her predecessor, Lula.[23]

The chill in relations extended beyond the diplomatic sphere. Trade likewise became a casualty of cooling ties. In 2010, for example, Brazil purchased $123.3 million in Iranian products, but in 2013 imports only totaled $8.3 million—a 93.3 percent reduction. Exports of Brazilian products to Iran, meanwhile, similarly declined, from $2.1 billion in 2010 to $1.6 billion in 2013.[24] Current trade volume between the two countries is lower still, and just a fraction of what it was under Lula.

Without the privileged access that was granted during the Lula era, Iranian officials attempted a "private" diplomatic offensive to try to regain ground lost with the new government. In June 2012, for example, then-Iranian President Mahmoud Ahmadinejad attempted to use the UN Conference on Sustainable Development in Rio de Janeiro to jumpstart relations by approaching officials in the Rousseff government and leaders of Brazil's private sector. But the effort showed little tangible result.[25]

Historically, Brazil has been an important trading partner for Iran, and its largest trade partner in the region; today, however, Iran has little relevance to the Brazilian economy. While Iranian officials point to President Dilma Rousseff as the point of contention, the Brazilian perspective is that the clear nuclear intentions of Ahmadinejad, his polarizing rhetoric towards the West, along with the flagrant human rights violations on behalf of the Islamic Republic, forced the Dilma government to take a more prudent stance. Any ideological kinship shared with the Iranian government, was supplanted with the need to show diplomatic and political maturity on the world stage, particularly as Brazil prepared to host two of the largest international sporting events (the 2014 FIFA World Cup and the 2016 Summer Olympics).

Although the reversal of policy executed by the Rousseff administration represented a severe blow to Iran's standing and objectives in South America, the continued placement of radical groups working as proxies for Tehran has continued apace in Brazil. These cells are disguised as cultural centers, charitable associations, and religious groups. Many of the members of these cells underwent training in Iran and operate below the radar in Brazil (although not unbeknownst to Brazilian officials) and preach radical Islam, anti-Zionism, and the destruction of Western culture from within Brazil's borders.

This continued asymmetric presence has recently been combined with increased diplomatic dialogue between the Brazilian parliament and delegates of the new Iranian president Hassan Rouhani. With Iran currently negotiating the direction of its nuclear program in Geneva, and the United States embracing a softer stance and at least a partial rollback of sanctions on the Islamic Republic, this has presented a window of opportunity for Iran to reengage Brazil in hopes of enhancing bilateral relations.

In July 2013, just before Rouhani was inaugurated, the Iranian ambassador to Brazil, Ali Ghazenadeh, announced that the new president would work toward rebuilding diplomatic ties between Iran and Brazil. Ghazenadeh offered an invitation to Brazil to begin talks on issues of technology and energy exploration. In February 2014, less than a year later, the president of Iran's parliament, Ali Larijani, and the Chairman of the Iranian Parliament's National Security and Foreign Policy Commission, Alaeddin Boroujerdi, welcomed a contingent of four high-ranking Brazilian congressmen, selected from among the parties that support Dilma's government, to re-establish ties between the two countries.[26]

These talks are seen as initial steps to re-establish a once-burgeoning bilateral relationship. While Brazil engages in diplomatic dialogue, it continues to deny the fact that Islamic extremism is present and active in the Federative Republic, and that Iranian-supported Hezbollah militants and other terrorists are recruiting, raising funds, and proselytizing within Brazil's borders. If Brazil's upcoming general election (slated for October 2014) results in the re-election of Rousseff and, perhaps more importantly, a continued majority for the Workers' Party within the Brazilian parliament, Iran will have the latitude to continue to carefully and gradually sway Brazil back into its geopolitical orbit.

NOTES

1. Israel Security Agency, "Terrorist Attack Against the Embassy of Israel in Buenos Aires, Argentina (1992)," n.d., http://www.shabak.gov.il/English/History/Affairs/Pages/ TerroristEmbassyes1992.aspx.

2. Alejandro Rúa, "Comision Interamericana de Derechos Humanos," Unidad Especial De Investigación Ministerio De Justicia Y Derechos Humanos República Argentina (2005), https:/ /www2.jus.gov.ar/Amia/pdf/presentacion040305.pdf.

3. Duncan Campbell, "Iran Was behind 1994 Argentina Bombing, Says Defector," *Guardian* (London), July 23, 2002, http://www.guardian.co.uk/world/2002/jul/23/iran. duncancampbell.

4. Departmento Unidad de Investigacion Antiterrorista de la Policia Federal Argentina, "Difusion de Imagenes Fotograficas," July 18, 1995, https://www2.jus.gov.ar/Amia/ DifusionImagenes.htm.

5. Raul Kollmann, "La Pieza Clave En La Teoría Del Fiscal," En La Causa por El Ataque a la AMIA, La Fiscalia Pidio la Detencion de un Colombiano, May 12, 2009, http://prensa. cancilleria.gov.ar/noticia.php?id=18094632.

6. Leonardo Coutinho, "A Rede o Terror Finca Bases no Brasil," *Veja* (Sao Paulo), April 6, 2011, http://veja.abril.com.br/acervodigital/?cod=JMRRGRRPEQI.

7. Ibid.

8. "Diário Oficial Da União (DOU)," *JusBrasil*, June 8, 2009, http://www.jusbrasil.com. br/diarios/768112/dou-secao-1-06-08-2009-pg-32; "Diário Oficial Da União (DOU)," *JusBrasil*, December 12, 2011, http://www.jusbrasil.com.br/diarios/33068976/dou-secao-1-12-12-2011-pg-171.

9. Coutinho, "A Rede o Terror Finca Bases No Brasil."

10. Rodrigo Randel, "'Professor' Terrorista," *Veja* (Sao Paulo), April 20, 2011, http://veja. abril.com.br/acervodigital/home.aspx?cod=JMRRGQRPMNO.

11. Rodrigo Jalloul, "Minha Historia," *UOL*, July 27, 2011, http://www1.folha.uol.com.br/ fsp/mundo/ft2707201113.htm.

12. Randel, "'Professor' Terrorista."

13. Samy Adghirni, "Radicado no Irã, Rodrigo Jalloul é o 1o brasileiro nato a se tornar clérico xiita," *Folho de Sao Paulo*, March 13, 2013, http://www1.folha.uol.com.br/mundo/ 2013/03/1245309-radicado-no-ira-o-paulistano-rodrigo-jalloul-e-o-1-brasileiro-nato-a-se-tornar-clerigo-xiita.shtml.

14. Lucas Ferraz, "PF Confirma Ligação De Libanês Com Al Qaeda," *UOL*, July 8, 2009, http://www1.folha.uol.com.br/folha/mundo/ult94u592241.shtml.

15. Valéria De Oliveira, "Terroristas Já Recrutam Brasileiros, Diz PF Em Audiência Convocada Por Jungmann," *PPS 23*, July 8, 2009, http://portal.pps.org.br/portal/showData/153723.

16. U.S. Department of the Treasury, "Treasury Targets Hizballah Financial Network," September 12, 2010, http://www.treasury.gov/press-center/press-releases/Pages/tg997.aspx.

17. Tom Cooper, Farzad Bishop, and Cláudio Lucchesi, "O Tucano no Irã. Revista Asas: revista de cultura e história da aviação," *Brasília* (DF) 5, no. 30, April–May 2006, 62–65.

18. "Entrevista—Roberto Abdenur," *Fazenda*, September 6, 2010, http://www.fazenda. gov.br/resenhaeletronica/MostraMateria.asp?page= andcod=663357.

19. "Memorando De Entendimento Entre O Governo Da República Federativa Do Brasil E O Governo Da República Islâmica Do Irã Para Cooperação Em Geologia, Mineração E Industrias De Transformação Mineral," May 16, 2010, http://dai-mre.serpro.gov.br/atos-internacionais/bilaterais/2010/memorando-de-entendimento-entre-o-governo-da-republica-federativa-do-brasil-e-o-governo-da-republica-islamica-do-ira-para-cooperacao-em-geologia-mineracao-e-industrias-de-transformacao-mineral/.

20. Ibid.

21. Roger Noriega, "Com Apoio Do Irã, Chávez Inicia Seu Programa Nuclear,"*Estadao.com.br*, October 10, 2010, http://www.estadao.com.br/noticias/impresso,com-apoio-do-ira-Chávez-inicia-seu-programa-nuclear,623090,0.htm.

22. "Diplomata Iraniano Diz Que Pressão Fez Brasil "mudar" Com Irã," *R7 Noticias*, March 26, 2011, http://noticias.r7.com/internacional/noticias/diplomata-iraniano-diz-que-pressao-fez-brasil-mudar-com-ira-20110326.html.

23. "Porta-voz De Ahmadinejad Critica Dilma E Diz Que Relações Entre Irã E Brasil Foram Afetadas Sob O Governo Da Presidente," *Zero Hora* Clic RBS, January 23, 2012, http://zerohora.clicrbs.com.br/rs/economia/noticia/2012/01/porta-voz-de-ahmadinejad-critica-dilma-e-diz-que-relacoes-entre-ira-e-brasil-foram-afetadas-sob-o-governo-da-presidente-3640303.html.

24. Ministério Do Desenvolvimento, Indústria E Comércio Exterior, "Balanca Comercial Brasiliera Fevereiro 2013—3 Semana," February 2014, http://www.desenvolvimento.gov.br/sitio/interna/interna.php?area=5andmenu=567.

25. Marc Humphries, "Rare Earth Elements: The Global Supply Chain." Congressional Research Service *CRS Report for Congress* (2012), http://www.fas.org/sgp/crs/natsec/R41347.pdf; "Ree In Military Application." Cache Exploration Inc., n.d, http://www.cacheexploration.com/index.php/ree-in-military-application.

26. "Iran, Brazil Underline Consolidation of Ties," FARS (Tehran), February 18, 2014, http://english.farsnews.com/newstext.aspx?nn=13921129000674.

Chapter Six

Sanctions Busting Schemes in Ecuador

Alex Pérez*

Until quite recently, Iran faced extensive economic pressure from the international community over its nuclear program. Over the past decade-and-a-half, the United States and its European allies painstakingly erected an extensive array of economic mechanisms aimed at isolating and imposing costs on the Islamic Republic for its nuclear activities. In response, the Iranian regime sought to build new economic ties with various nations as a way of lessening its international isolation. Latin America has figured prominently in this calculus, and Iran's strategic penetration of the region has included a significant economic dimension.

Over the past two decades, sanctioned Iranian funds have found their way into financial institutions in Venezuela, Ecuador, and Panama, through a variety of channels and methods. However, no method has been more ambitious than the relatively recent scheme to use an emerging Latin American monetary system called the *Sistema Único de Compensación Regional*, or SUCRE, as a platform to evade sanctions. The SUCRE is a proposed regional currency that is currently being used as a virtual accounting unit in commercial exchange between members of the anti-U.S. regional bloc known as the Bolivarian Alliance of the Americas (ALBA). [1]

Implementation of the SUCRE opens the door for Iran to shield its financial activities in Latin America, as the central banks of ALBA countries can utilize the SUCRE to bypass international financial authorities without having to rely on U.S. correspondent accounts. This illicit financial relationship between Iran and ALBA has been years in the making, originating in Venezuela through a "nesting" scheme that was later exposed, and which subsequently morphed into a state-sponsored trade-based money-laundering scheme using public and private banks in Ecuador. Frequent high-level official visits between the two countries have yielded numerous deals to inject

51

Iranian funds into the U.S. and European financial systems via Latin America.

Because the SUCRE is a "virtual currency," it is potentially the perfect tool for Iran to skirt international authorities. And while sanctions pressure on Iran has lessened somewhat in recent months as a result of its negotiations with U.S. and European powers over its nuclear program, there is ample evidence to suggest that the Iranian regime is consolidating its international money-laundering network, and increasing its commercial footprint throughout Latin America through a maze of Iranian front companies.

IRAN'S FAILED "NESTING" SCHEME IN VENEZUELA

Utilizing the SUCRE as a parallel financial system could be Iran's most sophisticated financial scheme in Latin America to date. But it is far from the Islamic Republic's first attempt to establish a financial foothold in the region.

Iran's first major attempt to circumvent sanctions by utilizing Latin American financial institutions began on January 2, 2008, with the inauguration of the *Banco Internacional de Desarrollo C.A. Banco Universal* (BID) in Venezuela. At first blush, the BID appeared to be a regular financial institution opening its doors in Caracas, but upon closer examination by the U.S. Department of Treasury's Office of Foreign Assets and Controls (OFAC), it was discovered to be wholly owned by the infamous *Toseyeh Saderat Iran Bank,* making it an independent subsidiary of the Export Development Bank of Iran (EDBI). This earned the BID the designation of Specially Designated National (SDN) on OFAC's targeted sanctions list in October of that same year, effectively freezing its assets and prohibiting transactions with U.S. parties.[2] In 2010, the European Union further sanctioned the Venezuelan BID and froze the remainder of its funds in Europe, as well as proscribing it from obtaining additional resources.

The name of the Venezuelan subsidiary is curiously similar to the *Banco Interamericano de Desarrollo*, the legitimate regional banking organization based out of Washington, D.C. The Washington-based BID engages in a number of daily financial transactions with a multitude of financial entities throughout the region. Utilizing the same initials—BID—for Venezuela's *Banco Internacional de Desarrollo* was a fairly obvious attempt to confuse U.S. financial entities on transactions and manifests, and to deflect suspicion from its activities.

This is not an uncommon scheme in the world of international money laundering. The widely utilized tactic known as "nesting" is fairly simple and effective. Iran would use Venezuelan banks, with ties to third party banks in the region that have longstanding relationships with U.S. financial institutions, in order to inject Iranian funds into the U.S. financial system. Most international wire transfers that are denominated in U.S. dollars are cleared through correspondent accounts abroad. At the time Iran's "nesting" scheme began, Venezuela was not under U.S. or international economic sanctions, so banks in the United States that process wire transfers from Venezuela relied almost exclusively on the Venezuelan bank to ensure the funds being transferred were legitimate.[3]

Aware of this vulnerability, Iran established a "nesting" scheme using the Venezuelan BID to gain access to the U.S. financial system by operating through a U.S. correspondent account belonging to another foreign financial institution in the region. The Venezuelan BID quickly established other banking relationships with mainstream commercial banks in Venezuela, such as *Banco Banesco*, as well as banks in Panama that have longstanding U.S. correspondent accounts. The result was that Iran obtained potential access to the U.S. financial system, due to the fact that the U.S. bank was unaware that its foreign correspondent customer (e.g., in Venezuela or Panama) was providing access to a sanctioned third party.[4]

Iran pursued this strategy aggressively between 2006 and 2008, even purportedly setting up additional chapters or affiliates of the Venezuelan BID in Bolivia, Brazil, and Ecuador.[5] This plan, however, was halted once sanctions were imposed on the principal entity in Venezuela. These sanctions were followed by others, levied against Venezuela's petroleum industry (*Petróleos de Venezuela*, PDVSA) and its defense industry (*Compañia Anónima Venezolana de Industrias Militar*, CAVIM) for dealings with Iran.[6] With the heat turned up in Venezuela, Iran was forced to shift its strategy in order to continue to launder its funds in the region. Shortly thereafter, Iran found an opportunity further south in the region, in Ecuador.

IRAN'S EMERGING FINANCIAL
RELATIONSHIP WITH ECUADOR

Since 2007, Ecuador has moved steadily away from the United States and closer to Venezuela, mostly due to the political rise of U.S.-trained economist Rafael Correa, the country's current president. As part of this process, Ecuador officially joined the ALBA bloc in June of 2009.[7]

With its dollarized economy and anti-American president, Ecuador provided Iran a secondary ingress into Latin America for its financial maneuvering. As of today, Ecuador has not been blacklisted by any international financial authority, and can operate freely within the international financial system. Moreover, Ecuador's economy has established ties to the U.S. financial system, making it an attractive partner for the Iranian regime.

On January 15, 2007, Iranian President Mahmoud Ahmadinejad and his then-Venezuelan counterpart, Hugo Chávez, visited Quito, the capital of

Ecuador, to attend the inauguration of incoming President Rafael Correa.[8] It is believed that during this visit the three discussed establishing a banking relationship between the Export Development Bank of Iran (EDBI) and the *Banco Central de Ecuador* (BCE). A year and a half later, in June 2008, an internal memo was produced by the BCE that explicitly mentioned the existing sanctions set forth on EDBI as a "high risk factor" for doing business with Iran. It was reported at the time that several mid-level managers at the BCE raised concerns about establishing such a risky relationship with the Islamic Republic. The most vocal among them was former General Manager Karina Saenz, who, despite being personally recruited by Correa, was staunchly opposed to any formal agreements between the BCE and Iran.[9]

Nevertheless, BCE issued a report on November 6, 2008, that suggested ways of mitigating the risks, and detailed a hypothetical system of payments that would enable financial transactions with the EDBI. This report was produced in advance of a December 2008 trip by President Correa and several high-ranking staffers of the BCE to Tehran.[10] During that visit, a host of new bilateral agreements were signed, including the establishment of reciprocal embassies. Most pertinent, however, was the signing of a "Protocol of Cooperation" between EDBI and the BCE on December 6, 2008. Among other provisions, it allowed the EDBI to extend $40 million in credit to the Central Bank of Ecuador for financing the importation of Iranian "goods and services." Mere days after the signing, the EDBI extended an additional $80 million (for a grand total of $120 million) as an initial line of credit for the BCE to request at an opportune time.[11]

The architect of this initial banking agreement with Iran was newly appointed BCE President Carlos Vallejo Lopez, a former agriculture minister who had only recently joined the Bank's institutional board. Vallejo was the main driver of the relationship with Iran within the BCE, and advocated strongly for Ecuador's emerging relationship with the Islamic Republic. He would resign in December 2009 from his position as BCE President, allegedly over tensions with Correa over a missed deadline to complete a reserves transfer to public-sector banks in Ecuador. But Vallejo's alleged tension with Correa did not last long; he was named the new Ambassador to Italy just a few months later (in February 2010).[12] Vallejo remains one of the staunchest defenders and public advocates for the Iran-Ecuador relationship.

Vallejo's successor at the BCE was an unlikely candidate: Diego Borja. A trained economist who previously served as Finance Minister (and more recently in the prestigious position of Coordinating Minister of Economic Policy of Ecuador), Borja had an ambivalent position toward Iran's relationship with the BCE, and had even supported some of Karina Saenz's concerns. Indeed, a month before being officially confirmed as BCE President in March 2010, he traveled to Washington, D.C., to meet with representatives from the U.S. Treasury Department, Federal Reserve and International Monetary Fund to dispel myths about the Iran-Ecuador financial relationship. At the time, Borja pointed out that while a credit line had been established, no actual Iranian funds had been deposited into BCE accounts.[13] Borja's appointment thus put some U.S. officials at ease, but their relief would be short-lived. Borja's tenure as BCE President ended soon after, and in November 2011, he was appointed as the Economic Secretary of ALBA. His successor as head of the BCE, and its most recent president, is the cousin of Rafael Correa: Pedro Delgado.

Delgado also caused controversy with regard to Iran's financial relationship with Ecuador, but not because of his public role as president of the BCE. Rather, it was because of his private role as the head of a public trust that owned shares of the state-owned *Banco Cofiec* S.A. The *Corporación Financiera Ecuatoriana*, or the COFIEC Bank, was founded on November 30, 1965, by José Antonio Correa Escobar in order to create a financial entity in Ecuador that could loan money as well as take part in venture capital. After the Ecuadorian banking crisis of 1999, the COFIEC Bank was bought out by the state through Ecuador's insurance deposit agency, the *Agencia de Garantía de Depositos*, an autonomous entity directed by the Ministry of Economy and Finance.[14] The COFIEC Bank quickly came under suspicion by international financial authorities for its role as a principal commercial link between Iran and Ecuador, while Pedro Delgado came under fire in Ecuador for his role in authorizing an irregular $800,000 loan to an Argentine "investor" Gastón Duzac.[15]

In February of 2013, Pedro Delgado reportedly traveled to Moscow, Russia, with representatives of the COFIEC Bank to hold meetings with *Bank Melli Iran ZAO*, a wholly owned subsidiary of the infamous *Bank Melli*, one of Iran's principal financial institutions and one that is currently sanctioned by the United States, United Nations, and European Union for aiding and abetting Iran's WMD and missile programs. *Bank Melli's* subsidiary in Moscow is one of four throughout the world, with branches in London, Tehran, and Kabul. All are heavily involved with international money laundering in support of the Islamic Republic. It is unclear what Delgado and representatives of the COFIEC Bank discussed with representatives of *Bank Melli Iran ZAO*. But, immediately after leaving Moscow, the Ecuadorian delegation flew to Tehran to hold meetings with more private banks, which included *Saman Bank, Parsian Bank*, and most notably the *Pasargad Bank*, which is currently Iran's fastest growing private bank. All of these entities have been sanctioned by Treasury's OFAC, and the *Pasargad Bank* was added to the blacklist in July of 2012.

This is particularly important because *Pasargad* sent a request to the COFIEC Bank in late 2011, following the meetings in Tehran, to register its name internally in Ecuador's financial system on an account with an alternative currency.[16] This would require the COFIEC Bank to open accounts in third party countries in currencies other than the U.S. dollar. Hypothetically, once this alternative currency is in effect, both countries could start trading and *Pasargad* could wire funds through COFIEC's third party account(s).

A few months before Delgado's trip to Tehran, on October 10, 2011, the Constitutional Tribunal of Ecuador approved a trade agreement with Iran that facilitates a commercial relationship between Quito and the Islamic Republic.[17] Article 11 of this agreement establishes that payments between Iran and Ecuador will be made in "freely convertible currencies."[18] It is believed that this "freely convertible currency" is a reference to the "SUCRE," and that its use will facilitate Iran's scheme for laundering funds through Latin America's U.S.-connected financial system.

THE SUCRE AS AN ALTERNATIVE VIRTUAL CURRENCY

The idea for an alternative currency was initially promulgated at ALBA's Third Extraordinary Summit on November 26, 2008, in Caracas, Venezuela, and the formal agreement to establish the SUCRE was approved less than a year later. The SUCRE is composed of four components—a Regional Monetary Council (CMR), a Central Clearing Compensation Chamber, a Regional Trade and Reserves Convergence Fund, and a common unit of account—the *sucre* (lowercase).[19]

Up to this point, the SUCRE has been used as a virtual accounting system to denominate trade between ALBA nations. The mechanism for using the SUCRE is fairly straightforward:

- Each authorized operative bank within an ALBA member nation deposits funds (in their local currency) into a specific account within the central bank of their own country (e.g., Venezuela).
- The central bank of the host country then transfers the funds to a specific account in the central bank of the targeted country (e.g., Ecuador) through the Central Clearing Compensation Chamber, which serves as a clearinghouse.
- The clearinghouse converts the currency into *sucres* at an exchange rate of one *sucre* for every $1.25.
- The central bank in the targeted country (Ecuador) then converts the sucres into its local currency and credits the host country's account (Venezuela).[20]

Once SUCRE transactions are occurring with relative frequency, the value of the *sucre* is derived from a basket of currencies from member countries, weighted according to the relative size of their respective economies. This is similar to how the Euro was developed utilizing the European Currency Unit

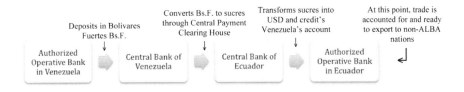

Figure 6.1. The SUCRE trade model (e.g., Venezuela to Ecuador)

as the basket of currencies of the European Community, which predates the European Union.[21]

Over the long term, the SUCRE is intended to replace the U.S. dollar as the primary medium of exchange in Latin America, in order to break the hegemony of the U.S. dollar in regional trade. Its first transactions as a virtual currency took place in 2010 between Venezuela and Ecuador, and in 2012 it reached $420 million in transactions. It is expected to reach close to $1 billion in total transactions since the beginning in 2010 to the end of the current year.[22] For the SUCRE to gain power, ALBA member countries will have to increasingly deposit their foreign reserves in an ALBA Bank denominated in *sucres*. In 2013, ten of the twelve ALBA countries agreed to deposit one percent of their international reserves into the ALBA Bank. While the ALBA bank controls the central clearinghouse, commercial entities must make deposits through their respective Central Banks, as depicted above.

Therein lies the importance of the banking agreement signed between Iran and Ecuador in 2008. Regardless of which ALBA nation decides to trade with Ecuador, this agreement affords Iran the ability to leverage its financial activity in Latin America through one principal entity, minimizing the risk. Moreover, it affords Iran the possibility of offsetting its accounts directly, without making use of correspondent banks abroad. The reliance on correspondent banks was one of the "high risk factors" with Iran's nesting scheme in Venezuela, which is why in the BCE report produced before Rafael Correa's visit to Tehran in December 2008 mentions alternative methods for engaging Iran, stating: "for this reason, we have analyzed other methods of payment in order to materialize commerce between the two nations" [editor's translation].

In order to engage in voluminous commercial activity, Iran will have to work with "Agent Banks" that are selected by ALBA's Regional Monetary Council. These Agent Banks are central to the operation of the SUCRE because they determine the terms of payment after the *sucres* are converted into a local currency by the respective Central Bank. Most of these Agent Banks are determined by bilateral and multilateral agreements with the Central Banks of the ALBA countries. The COFIEC Bank in Ecuador, for example, could be a typical Agent Bank that could facilitate Iranian funds moving

from Latin America into the United States (though it is not currently suspected of doing so).

It is notable that the agreement that laid the groundwork for Ecuador to
trade with Iran through an "alternative currency" was one of the last efforts
overseen by Diego Borja before he became ALBA's Economic Secretary. In
his new position, Borja is also the President of the Technical Commission of
the New International Financial Architecture, which is a somewhat grandiose
title that simply means that he will be overseeing the implementation of
ALBA's regional currency, the SUCRE, from a virtual accounting unit to a
hard currency.

During Diego Borja's trip to Washington, D.C., in 2012, he assured U.S.
officials that Ecuador had no plan to replace the U.S. dollar as its currency.
Yet, in subsequent meetings with UNASUR and other public outings, Borja
has repeated that it "makes no sense" for South American nations to use the
U.S. dollar over local currencies for regional trade, and in Ecuador he has
encouraged small- to medium-size enterprises to conduct commercial exchange in the *sucre*,[23] which would require them to become Agent Banks of
the BCE.

Despite all this maneuvering, there have been setbacks to the implementation of the SUCRE and the use of the COFIEC Bank in Ecuador. Most
notably, the COFIEC Bank has drawn negative attention to itself for providing irregular loans to third party nationals, thereby upsetting many Ecuadorean small business owners who have been denied loans by the COFIEC Bank
in the past. This has now been dubbed the "COFIEC case" or the "COFIEC
crisis" in Ecuador, and has resulted in significant media attention.[24] Moreover, the supposed brain behind the implementation of the SUCRE, Diego
Borja, was recently removed from his position as Economic Secretary of
ALBA due to a dispute with Ecuador's Foreign Minister, Ricardo Patiño.

Figure 6.2.   Iran's hypothetical penetration of SUCRE trade model

EMBEDDING INTO IRAN'S GLOBAL
MONEY-LAUNDERING NETWORK

This emerging virtual monetary system in Latin America has the potential to be used for a variety of international money-laundering schemes. And while it is currently in its infancy, the system is rapidly evolving and appears to be a priority for the ALBA bloc as it moves into the post-Chávez era. Iran's preferential banking relationships with central banks in Venezuela and Ecuador affords it the opportunity to use this system as a way to skirt U.S. and international sanctions and evade financial authorities.

Iran's decision to turn to Latin America to launder its money and gain access to international financial systems should come as no surprise. According to the Inter-American Development Bank, money-laundering activity in Latin America is possibly the highest in the world, with between 2.5 and 6.3 percent of the region's gross domestic product being "washed" through a variety of laundering schemes.[25] Both the Paris-based Financial Action Task Force (FATF) and the U.S.-based Financial Crimes Enforcement Network (FinCEN) place Ecuador and Venezuela among the highest risk countries in the region for money laundering or terrorist financing.

Much of the money laundering in Latin America accrues to the benefit of high-end drug trafficking organizations that "layer" their funds into a variety of financial institutions in those regions. These networks have been established for quite some time, and Ecuador has become a hub for drug trafficking in recent years.

Currently, there are signs that indicate that Iran may be consolidating its international money-laundering network to synchronize with their new Latin American allies. Prior to arriving in Moscow on February 2013, Pedro Delgado is known to have had stopovers in London and Austria. The latter is reportedly a hub for Iran's money laundering efforts in Europe, and the former is a hotbed for subversive activity that caused British officials to close the Iranian embassy in London in November of 2011.[26]

Moreover, after Canada ejected Iranian diplomats and closed down their embassy in 2012, a number of officials suspected that it was because of Iran's money laundering activities that supported subversive activities in Ottawa, the Greater Toronto Area (GTA) and elsewhere in the country.[27] One of the Iranian diplomats formerly stationed in Canada, Hassan Doutagi, was reassigned to Quito to become the *Ministro Consejero* (equivalent to Deputy Chief of Mission) for the Iranian mission in Ecuador after the Iranian embassy in Ottawa was closed down.[28]

Iran's international money-laundering operations have utilized alternative banking systems or virtual currencies in the past. Several reports have been released in recent years indicating that Iran was continually searching for countries to develop alternative banking relationships to hide from American and European spy agencies and international monitoring bodies. Armenia, a former Soviet satellite state, is allegedly using some of its larger full-service financial institutions (with long-standing relationships in Europe) to inject sanctioned Iranian funds into the European market.[29] Historically, Turkey and the United Arab Emirates (UAE) have been Iran's principal banking connections to Europe, but both have been under intense pressure from the international community to cut their banking ties with Tehran.

More recently, the virtual currency BITCOIN—developed by the mysterious Japenese tech guru Satoshi Nakamoto—has become a target of Iranian attention due to the fact that it can easily be exchanged for physical currencies like Euros or dollars. One of the online sites that facilitate this exchange is the Finland-based localbitcoins.com, whose founder was quoted as saying: "I believe bitcoin is, or will be in the future, a very effective tool for individuals who want to avoid sanctions, currency restrictions, and high inflation in countries such as Iran."[30]

Consequently, Iran's money-laundering operations in Latin America appear to be part of a global effort to find alternative avenues to avoiding sanctions. United Nations Security Council Resolution 1747 (UNSCR 1747), along with additional sanctions by the United States and European Union, have sought to close off Iran's access to high-end materials and technology that can support its nuclear and WMD programs. Yet, Iran's money-laundering schemes have nonetheless succeeded in procuring black market materiel, technology, and equipment from Europe, Africa and more recently Asia. Its international laundering network has seen success using a maze of entities, aliases and shell companies to deceive banks into processing payments to acquire banned "dual-use" goods. The aforementioned Latin American money-laundering operations provide additional methods to skirt what have become predictable sanctions.

Today, diplomatic negotiations with the United States and European powers have somewhat lessened Iran's need for such arrangements. However, Iran's financial engagement in Latin America is still notable because of its ability to provide the Islamic Republic with alternative and much-needed economic vibrancy should sanctions be re-imposed—and because Iran's exploitation of Latin American markets tracks closely with the efforts by regional leaders, like Ecuador's Correa, to create an alternative political and economic system in the region.

NOTES

*Alex Pérez is a pseudonym for an analyst that worked on this chapter in cooperation with the Centro de Análisis e Investigación Internacional (CENAIN) based in Quito.

1. Joel Hirst, "A Guide to ALBA: What Is the Bolivarian Alternative to the Americas and What Does It Do?" *Americas Quarterly*, March 2012, http://www.americasquarterly.org/hirst/article.

2. U.S. Department of Treasury, Office of Foreign Assets Control, "Recent OFAC Actions," October 22, 2008, http://www.treasury.gov/resource-center/sanctions/OFAC-Enforcement/pages/20081022.aspx.

3. Author interviews with officials in the U.S. Department of Treasury, October 2012.

4. Robert M. Morgenthau, "The Emerging Axis of Iran and Venezuela," *Wall Street Journal*, September 8, 2009, http://online.wsj.com/article/SB10001424052970203440104574400792835972018.html.

5. A "Protocol of Cooperation" was signed between EDBI (Iran) and BCE (Ecuador) where a mention of EDBI's "readiness to establish a branch of Banco International de Desarrollo (BID) in the Republic of Ecuador, and BCE paves the way for expedition of such an act."

6. Frank López Ballesteros, "Venezuela acumula diez sanciones de EEUU y la UE," *El Universal* (Caracas), May 29, 2011, http://www.eluniversal.com/2011/05/29/venezuela-acumula-diez-sanciones-de-eeuu-y-la-ue.shtml.

7. Joel Hirst, *The ALBA: Inside Venezuela's Bolivarian Alliance* (CreateSpace Independent Publishing Platform, 2012).

8. Jose R. Cardenas, "Meet Latin America's Next Hugo Chávez," *Washington Times*, April 6, 2012, http://www.washingtontimes.com/news/2012/apr/6/meet-latin-americas-next-hugo-Chávez/.

9. Wikileaks cable dated December 22, 2009, "Subj: Ecuador Gradually Solidifies Relationship with Iran's Export Development Bank," http://www.eluniverso.com/2011/04/12/1/1355/cable-241300.html.

10. Jose Cardenas, "The Chávez Model Threatens Ecuador," American Enterprise Institute *Latin America Outlook*, March 21, 2011, http://www.aei.org/article/foreign-and-defense-policy/regional/latin-america/the-chvez-model-threatens-ecuador/.

11. Author interviews with former officers in Ecuador's military intelligence, December 2011. The document in question is currently in author's possession.

12. "Carlos Vallejo nombrado embajador de Ecuador en Italia," *El Hoy* (Quito), February 26, 2010, http://www.hoy.com.ec/noticias-ecuador/carlos-vallejo-nombrado-embajador-de-ecuador-en-italia-394847.html.

13. Wikileaks cable dated March 3, 2009, "Subj: New Coordinating Minister for Economic Policy Borja," http://www.eluniverso.com/2011/04/24/1/1355/cable-195027.html.

14. Francisco Rosales Ramos, "Cofiec," *El Hoy* (Quito), October 15, 2012, http://www.hoy.com.ec/noticias-ecuador/cofiec-563956.html.

15. Otto J. Reich, "Iran May Be 'Laundering' Money in Ecuadorian Banks," *Newsmax*, July 18, 2012, http://www.newsmax.com/Newsfront/Iran-Ecuador-money-laundering/2012/07/18/id/445807.

16. Ibid.

17. Author interviews with Ecuadorean Congressman, January 2011. The document in question is currently in author's possession.

18. Otto J. Reich and Ezequiel Vázquez Ger, "Iran's Stealth Financial Partners in Latin America," *Miami Herald*, March 14, 2012, http://www.newsmax.com/Newsfront/Iran-Ecuador-money-laundering/2012/07/18/id/445807.

19. Hirst, *The ALBA*.

20. A. Rosales, "El Banco del Sur y el SUCRE: (des) Acuerdos sobre una Arquitectura Financiera Alternativa," *Jornadas de Economia Critica*, February 15, 2010.

21. T. Kokkol, ed. *The Payment System: Payments, Securities and Derivatives, and the Role of the Eurosystem* (Frankfurt am Mian: European Central Bank, 2010).

22. "ALBA Members Trade \$420m with SUCRE January–September 2012," *Wall Street Journal*, September 20, 2012, http://online.wsj.com/article/BT-CO-20120920-711684.html.

23. Interview with Diego Borja, "La verdad sobre el sucre," *La Primera* (Lima), June 19, 2012, http://www.diariolaprimeraperu.com/online/especial/la-verdad-sobre-el-sucre_113605.html.

24. For a short summary of the "COFIEC Crisis," see Diego Araujo Sanchez "El escándalo de COFIEC," *El Hoy* (Quito), October 8, 2012, http://www.hoy.com.ec/noticias-ecuador/el-escandalo-de-cofiec-563382.html.

25. Eric Green, "Money Laundering Targeted as Menace to Latin America, Caribbean," IIP Digital, April 28, 2004, http://preprod.iipdigital.getusinfo.com/st/english/article/2004/04/20040428164024aeneerg0.6921045.html#axzz2E0WtQujz.

26. Damien McElroy, "Iranian Official 'Has Set Up International Money Laundering Network," *Telegraph* (London), October 21, 2012, http://www.telegraph.co.uk/news/worldnews/middleeast/iran/9624036/Iranian-official-has-set-up-international-money-laundering-network.html.

27. Michael Petrou, "Iran's Long Reach into Canada" *MacLean's*, June 20, 2012, http://www2.macleans.ca/2012/06/20/irans-long-reach-into-canada/.

28. Arturo Torres, "Occidente nos discrimina porque no seguimos las órdenes de EE.UU," *El Comercio* (Quito), September 25, 2012, http://www.elcomercio.com/mundo/Occidente-discrimina-seguimos-ordenes-EEUU_0_779922205.html.

29. Louis Charbonneau, "Iran Looks to Armenia to Skirt Bank Sanctions," Reuters, August 21, 2012, http://www.reuters.com/article/2012/08/21/us-iran-sanctions-armenia-idUSBRE87K05420120821.

30. Max Raskin, "Dollar-less Iranians Discover Virtual Currency," *Bloomberg Businessweek*, November 29, 2012, http://www.businessweek.com/articles/2012-11-29/dollar-less-iranians-discover-virtual-currency.

Chapter Seven

A Venezuelan Platform for Iran's Military Ambitions

Martin Rodil

Over the past decade, the Islamic Republic of Iran has intensified its activities in Latin America in an effort to counteract the international isolation that has resulted from the sweeping economic sanctions imposed against it by Western nations. Since 2005, Tehran has found favorable geopolitical conditions in the region for expanding its influence and evading international scrutiny surrounding its controversial nuclear program.

The Iranian presence in the Americas today extends to virtually all areas of politics and commerce, but in and of itself that does not represent a challenge to regional stability. However, Iran's historic support for international terrorism and its determined pursuit of nuclear weapons provide an ominous backdrop to its regional activities.

In this context, it is important to remember the words of the former Undersecretary for Terrorism and Financial Intelligence, Stuart Levy, who reminds us that these activities are supported by a "maze of financial entities" that "essentially hoodwink those still doing business with Iran into facilitating illicit transactions for the procurement and transport of dual-use, missile related items."[1] No better example of this web of covert activities and influence can be found than Iran's relations with Venezuela, which have provided the Islamic Republic a key foothold in the Western Hemisphere, and a latent capability to establish a military footprint there.

AN ALLY IN CARACAS

During his time in office (2005–2013), former Iranian president Mahmoud Ahmadinejad forged strong personal and political ties with his Venezuelan counterpart, Hugo Chávez—ties that the Iranian regime used to anchor itself in Latin America. Chávez in effect permitted his country to become a gateway into the region for Iran, and facilitated Iran's political outreach via the Bolivarian Alliance of the Americas (ALBA). Additionally, Chávez granted Iran access to various institutions of his "Bolivarian" state, and in doing so permitted the Islamic Republic to establish a firm foothold on Venezuelan territory.

The recent ties between Tehran and Caracas can be traced back to the rise of Ahmadinejad to the Iranian presidency in 2005. In the nine years since, the two governments have forged close political and economic ties, encompassing an estimated 262 bilateral agreements covering cooperation in the areas of commerce, industry, finance, agriculture and energy. These ties are not simply benign, however; a 2011 investigation carried out by the American Enterprise Institute in Washington, D.C., found that a large portion of the activities in those areas served Tehran for purposes other than those stated. [2]

A good example of this is Iran's use of financial projects for the laundering of assets and the evasion of international financial sanctions. Under a pattern developed and perfected in recent years, the Iranian government launched subsidiaries for front companies belonging to the Iranian Revolutionary Guard Corps in Venezuela, and channel their funds toward state owned energy firm *Petroleos de Venezuela S.A. (PDVSA)*. PDVSA then moves those funds through the local economy and, as a final step, has those funds injected into the international financial system.

Venezuelan financial institutions have also been co-opted and become complicit in such schemes. In just one example, the *Banco Internacional de Desarrollo C.A.*, a commercial Venezuelan bank wholly owned by Iran's Bank Saderat, was sanctioned in 2008 by the U.S. Treasury Department for its participation in the Iranian nuclear program. [3] Two years later, Bank Saderat was similarly sanctioned by the European Union because of suspicions that it was linked to Iran's nuclear effort. [4]

Another dual-use project is the arrangement between Venezuela's state-owned airline, *Conviasa S.A.* and the Islamic Republic's official Iran Air. Conviasa used to operate regular flights from Caracas to Damascus and Tehran—an air route that has been linked to drug transshipment and the transport of people, weapons, and other materials. [5] Once the flight arrives in Caracas or Tehran, custom authorities never inspect the Conviasa passengers or the cargo contents. During their years of operation, from 2007 to 2011, these flights were often "sold out"—with outside passengers unable to obtain a seat or able to do so only at prohibitive prices (approximately $2,000) that put tickets out of reach of ordinary Venezuelans.

Many analysts and U.S. law enforcement officials believed that the Conviasa and Iran Air code-share flight was used for the transportation of military technology from Iran to Venezuela. These suspicions were confirmed in

2009 when an anonymous website was created by Conviasa personnel who denounced the secrecy and exclusivity of these flights, and charged that missile system components and "radioactive materials" was being illegally transported.[6]

The joint venture tractor factory VENEIRAN in Venezuela's Bolivar State is yet another example of this type of collaboration. This industrial initiative has facilitated the transport of military equipment from Iran to Venezuela; in 2009, Turkish authorities uncovered the trafficking when they interdicted 22 containers loaded with undeclared military materiel in the port of Mersin.[7] The joint venture car factory VENIRAUTO is believed to play a similar role, given that it has only produced 15 percent of expected output in its eight years of existence.

DEFENSE-INDUSTRIAL COLLABORATION

Although the aforementioned projects represent potential challenges to regional security, the overt joint military activities of Iran and Venezuela—are even more alarming. Since 2008, two Iranian military enterprises—Parchin Chemical Industries and Qods Aviation Industries—have been established on Venezuelan territory, where they are developing joint military projects in collaboration with Venezuela's military industry, the *Compañia Anónima Venezolana de Industrias Militares* (CAVIM). These joint venture projects have Iranian military officers stationed in Venezuela and vice versa.

Parchin Chemical Industries (PCI) is part of Iran's Defense Industries Organization's Chemical Industries Group, and specializes in the production of ammunition, explosives, as well as the solid propellants for rockets and missiles. It is prominently listed in the annex to United Nations Security Council Resolution 1747, as an entity that is involved in Iran's missile and WMD programs. In April 2007, U.S. officials identified PCI "as the final recipient of sodium perchlorate monohydrate, a chemical precursor for solid propellant oxidizer, possibly to be used for ballistic missiles," and subsequently added them to the specially designated national and blocked persons list of the Department of Treasury's Office of Foreign Asset Control.[8]

In addition, the Parchin military complex approximately 20 kilometers southeast of Tehran (where PCI is believed to be located) is suspected to be a testing site for explosives used in the detonation of nuclear weapons. In Venezuela, PCI, alongside CAVIM is constructing nitroglycerine and nitrocellulose plants (both active ingredients for manufacturing explosives and propellants) as well as a gunpowder factory in the city of Moron, state of Falcón.[9]

For its part, Qods Aviation produces unmanned aerial vehicles, parachutes, gliders, and motors. In Maracay, in the Venezuelan state of *Aragua*, next to the Liberator Air Base, CAVIM and Qods are working together on a project for the production of unmanned aerial vehicles. Significantly, on January 30, 2011, a huge explosion rocked the Maracay plant and killed one person and caused damages to more than 3,400 homes. The results of the subsequent investigation carried out by the Military Prosecutor's Office were never revealed.[10] Like Parchin Chemical Industries, Qods Aviation is also sanctioned by the UN Security Council Resolution 1747, due to its involvement in the Iranian ballistic missile and nuclear programs.

A BOOMING ILLICIT TRADE

Iran's official shipping line, the Islamic Republic of Iran Shipping Lines (IRISL), is known to offer logistical solutions to the Defense and Logistics Department of the Armed Forces (MODAFL) of Iran and its subsidiary entities for the transportation of military cargo. As the United Nations has noted, the company facilitates shipments to known areas of proliferation, and does so by falsifying documentation and using deceptive schemes to cover up its involvement in such illicit trade.[11] In an effort to evade international sanctions, the company has started reflagging its ships—a tactic that has made it difficult for the international community to monitor its commerce. These maneuvers are part of a larger pattern of a behavior aimed at advancing Iran's nuclear and missile programs.

In Venezuela, IRISL makes use of Astinave, a shipyard that is close to *Centro de Refinación de Paraguaná* in the State of *Falcón*. This port has restricted access and its own Customs Office. The shipyard infrastructure was previously remodeled and expanded by the Iranian Offshore Engineering and Construction Company (IOEC), which now operates it. This company was sanctioned in 2011 by the European Union due to its participation in the construction of an uranium enrichment plant in Fordow, Iran.[12]

IRISL is part of a complicated logistical network for the transportation of military cargo between Iran and Venezuela. It works directly with the National Iranian Tanker Company (NITC), one of the largest tanker companies in the world. NITC contracts with *PDV Marina*, a subsidiary of PDVSA in charge of the distribution and transport of hydrocarbons. Through this network, Iran ensures that the products generated by its front companies and CAVIM are shipped from the Venezuelan port of Paraguaná to Tehran. The above arrangement implies that Venezuela plays an important role in the efforts of the Islamic Republic in acquiring military materiel otherwise denied to it by the international community.

Iran is likewise playing an active role in the Venezuelan port system and in the development of Venezuela's naval infrastructure far beyond the Paraguaná peninsula. The Iran Marine Industrial Company (SADRA), for example, has offices in Tehran, Caracas, and Puerto Cabello (the main commercial port and base of the Venezuelan Navy). SADRA is the leading company in Iran that carries out ship construction and repair. It, in turn, is known to generate funds that finance the operations of Iran's Revolutionary Guard Corps.

SADRA is also involved in the development of oilfields and gas deposits, and specializes in the construction of ships, docks, and floating oil platforms. Recently, it just completed the construction and delivered the first of four "Aframax" class oil tankers in Venezuela, and is in charge of the expansion of the DIANCA shipyard in Puerto Cabello. SADRA has been sanctioned by the Treasury Department's Office of Foreign Assets Control (OFAC) for being a part of *Khataam al-Anbiya*, the construction arm of the IRGC. [13]

Between 2009 and 2011, the Chávez regime provided still more evidence of it's illicit trade with Iran when General Aref Richany Jiménez simultaneously served as the Director of External Relations at PDVSA and as head of CAVIM, the military-industrial arm of Venezuela. Both, PDVSA and CAVIM, are currently under U.S. sanctions for its illicit trade with Iran.

A BEACHHEAD IN THE AMERICAS

This same timeframe, 2009 to 2011, was also notable for its sharp increase of improperly documented Iranian migrants traveling up north through the Western Hemisphere (namely to Canada) via Caracas. [14] Venezuela was a top embarkation point for these individuals because of the close relationship between their respective intelligence services.

Award-winning investigative journalist, Sebastian Rotella of ProPublica described this as a joint intelligence program between the respective Iranian and Venezuelan intelligence agencies. Sourcing Western intelligence officials, Rotella states that Venezuela agreed "to provide systematic help to Iran with intelligence infrastructure such as arms, identification documents, bank accounts and pipelines for moving operatives and equipment between Iran and Latin America." [15]

While many analysts have commented on Iran's use of such pipelines to propagate terrorist networks in Latin America, citing most infamously the 1994 AMIA attack in Argentina, few have made note of Iran's increasing military footprint in the region. Aside from serving as a regional hub for Iranian-proxy Hezbollah in the region, Venezuelan territory also serves as a base for Iranian intelligence and military officials who provide command and control support to more sophisticated projects in the region that establish plausible deniability for Iran's military ambitions.

The potential dual-use nature of many of Iran's projects in Venezuela, from their commercial endeavors to its overt military ventures, provides a glimpse into what these ambitions might be. General James R. Clapper, the Director of National Intelligence, noted in 2013 that "Iran may be more willing to seize opportunities to attack in the United States in response to perceived offenses against the regime."[16] Iran's strategic position in Venezuela, and its freedom of action there, can help to facilitate such an attack.

THE POST-CHÁVEZ ERA

The passing of Hugo Chávez on March 5, 2013, has brought with it much speculation about the future of his chief political project, the ALBA bloc, and by extension regarding Venezuela's relations with Iran. As of this writing, approximately a year after Chávez's demise, Venezuela is reaping the ramifications of more than a decade of disastrous economic policies. Nicolas Maduro, Chávez's handpicked protégé and Venezuela's current president, faces real constraints within its borders that prevent him from assuming any type of leadership role on the international stage.

This, however, can actually serve to bolster Venezuela's ties with Iran. As opposed to Chávez, who couched his relationship with Iran out of admiration for a fellow "revolutionary" anti-American regime, Maduro's relationship with Iran is very much one of necessity. At a time of austerity and shortages, Venezuela cannot afford to lose any trade partners, much less those that have already staked interest in Venezuela's lucrative energy sector. Maduro, who formerly served as foreign minister, has the relationships necessary to increase Venezuela's interaction with Iran and—against the backdrop of slackening international sanctions against the Islamic Republic—now has every incentive to do so.

Iran, meanwhile, is operating under a similar calculus. After years of investments in Venezuela, the Iranian regime will not let its stake in Venezuela go to waste. To this end, Iran's new president, Hassan Rouhani, has declared that his country wants to expand its relations with Latin America, and that Cuba and Venezuela are key to this effort.[17] Indeed, as of this writing, the Iranian government had already dispatched top diplomats to Venezuela to rekindle the relationship, indicating that strategic ties between Tehran and Caracas are hardly a thing of the past.

NOTES

1. U.S. Department of Treasury. (September 17, 2008). "Treasury Designated Iranian Military Firms" (http://www.treasury.gov/press-center/press-releases/Pages/hp1145.aspx).

2. On (November 14, 2011). "Iran's Threat in the Western Hemisphere" (http://www.aei.org/files/2011/11/14/-event-presentation-on-iran-in-the-western-hemisphere-roger-noriega_090836248875.pdf).

3. U.S. Department of the Treasury. (October 22, 2008). "Recent OFAC Actions" (http://www.treasury.gov/resource-center/sanctions/OFAC-Enforcement/pages/20081022.aspx).

4. Infobae.com (July 27, 2010). "The European Union Froze Funds of a Venezuelan Bank Due to Links with Iran" (http://www.infobae.com/notas/528341-La-Union-Europea-c ongelo-los-fondos-de-un-banco-venezolano-por-sus-vinculos-con-Iran.html).

5. La Stampa (Italia). (December 21, 2008). "Patto Caracas-Teheran Aerei in Cambio di Armi." (http://media.noticias24.com/0812/sta21.html).

6. El Pais (Spain). (November 23, 2009). "Caracas-Damasco-Teherán, un vuelo de lo más misterioso" (http://elpais.com/diario/2009/11/23/internacional/1258930803_850215.html).

7. AP/Israel News. (January 6, 2009). "Turkey Holds Suspicious Iran-Venezuela Shipment" (http://www.ynetnews.com/articles/0,7340,L-3651706,00.html).

8. U.S. Department of Treasury. (July 8, 2008). "Treasury Designates Iranian Proliferation Individuals, Entities" (http://www.treasury.gov/press-center/press-releases/Pages/hp1071.aspx).

9. Univision News. (January 13, 2012). "The Mysterious Venezuelan-Iranian Gunpowder Plant" (http://news.univision.com/article/2012-01-13/the-mysterious-venezuelan-iranian-gun powder-plant-casto-ocando).

10. Washington Times. (July 4, 2012). "Iranian Weapon's on America's Doorstep" (http://www.washingtontimes.com/news/2012/jul/4/iranian-weapons-on-americas-doorstep/?page=all).

11. United Nations Security Council 6335th Meeting. (June 9, 2010). "Security Council Imposes Additional Sanctions on Iran, Voting 12 in Favour to 2 Against, with 1 Abstention" (http://www.un.org/News/Press/docs/2010/sc9948.doc.htm).

12. Official Journal of the European Union. (December 1, 2011). "Council Decision 2011/783/CFSP" (http//eurlex.europa.eu/LexUriServ/LexUriServ.do?uri=OJ:L:2011:319:0071:009 1:EN:PDF).

13. U.S. Department of the Treasury. (March 28, 2012). "Treasury Announces Additional Sanctions against Iranian Engineering and Shipping Firms" (http://www.treasury.gov/press-center/press-releases/Pages/tg1509.aspx).

14. As detailed in Joseph M. Humire, testimony before the U.S. House Homeland Security Committee Subcommittee on Oversight and Management Efficiency (July 9, 2013).

15. ProPublica. (July 11, 2013). "The Terror Threat and Iran's Inroads in Latin America" (http://www.propublica.org/article/the-terror-threat-and-irans-inroads-in-latin-america).

16. As detailed in James R. Clapper, testimony before the Senate Select Committee on Intelligence titled "Worldwide Threat Assessment of the U.S. Intelligence Community" (March 12, 2013). (http://www.intelligence.senate.gov/130312/clapper.pdf).

17. MercoPress. (August 5, 2013). "Iran After Closer Relations with Latin America, Says New President Rouhani" (http://en.mercopress.com/2013/08/05/iran-after-closer-relations-with-latinamerica-says-new-president-rouhani).

Chapter Eight

A Bolivian Base for Iran's Military Advisors

Adrián Oliva

It was a warm autumn day on May 31, 2011, in the small town of Warnes, Bolivia, when Iran's Defense Minister, Brigadier General Ahmad Vahidi, arrived to inaugurate the new regional defense school for the Bolivarian Alliance of the Americas (ALBA). This would have been uneventful, except for the fact that the International Criminal Police Organization (INTERPOL) has a "red notice" out on Vahidi for his involvement in the infamous 1994 bombing in Buenos Aires of the AMIA Jewish community center. His arrival outraged both the regional Jewish community and Argentine authorities, which demanded his immediate extradition to Buenos Aires. The Bolivian government apologized, pled ignorance, and released a formulaic official statement condemning terrorism, but nevertheless allowed Vahidi to beat a hasty retreat back to Iran.

The Vahidi visit shed light on the burgeoning alliance between Bolivia and Iran—one that extends beyond the scope of the bilateral agreements agreed to by Tehran and La Paz. The new ALBA regional defense school was intended to provide political and ideological training to military leaders, while instructing civilian leaders in the art of asymmetric military strategy. To date, the school has not become fully operational. However, Iranian military advisors continue to arrive to this Andean nation. Consequently, as the ALBA bloc transitions into a post-Chávez era, Bolivia is quickly becoming a base for Iran's asymmetric operations throughout South America.

THE GEOPOLITICAL CONTEXT

The end of the Cold War was a landmark event for Latin America. The fall of the Berlin Wall in 1991 and the subsequent demise of Soviet global influence created a political vacuum that prompted a crisis for the traditional left in the Americas. The region responded with the creation of the *Foro de Sao Paulo*.[1] Founded in 1990 by the Brazilian Labor Party and the Cuban Communist Party, the *Foro* brought together some sixty regional political organizations with the objective of "redefining the goals and activities of the Latin American left after the fall of the Berlin Wall and the collapse of the Soviet Union."

Regrettably, this umbrella organization has played a fundamental role in the subsequent acquisition of political power by its members, often through dubious partnerships. Although the *Foro* officially opposes terrorism and violence, it has aligned itself with various NGOs and armed guerrilla movements, most notably the Revolutionary Armed Forces of Colombia (FARC) and Peru's *Sendero Luminoso* (Shining Path).

Since its founding, and particularly since the turn of the century, the *Foro* has grown in size and influence in Latin America. It has aided the ascent to power of numerous leftist Latin American governments, and in the process affected not only domestic politics in these nations but also the shape of regional and international institutions across the Western Hemisphere. Member groups of the *Foro de Sao Paulo* have established growing influence over the Organization of American States (OAS). Simultaneously, the *Foro* has created its own institutions, such as the Union of South American Nations (UNASUR), the Bolivarian Alliance of the Americas (ALBA) and, more recently, the Community of Latin American and Caribbean States (CELAC). Each of these has a different purpose, composition, and political character. But it is ALBA, whose members include Cuba, Venezuela, Bolivia, Ecuador, Nicaragua, and a handful of Caribbean satellite states, that has arguably achieved the greatest success—as well as the most extreme leftist orientation.

The regional integration promoted by the *Foro de Sao Paulo* and implemented by ALBA reinforced the need for the Latin American left to consolidate its security and defense apparatus. On February 5, 2012, Bolivian President Evo Morales and his then-Venezuelan counterpart, Hugo Chávez, proposed to do just that with the creation of a Defense Council at the XI ALBA Summit for Heads of States.[2] The move was not a surprise; the inauguration of the Warnes regional defense school the previous year had both foreshadowed and laid the groundwork for such a council. Together, both initiatives aimed to unify the strength and capabilities of smaller countries and ALBA member states while creating a joint military doctrine for the "new" Latin American left.

ALBA'S REGIONAL DEFENSE SCHOOL

The idea for the ALBA regional defense school was first conceived during the VII ALBA Summit hosted by Bolivia on October 2009. During that summit, ALBA leaders approved the creation of a *Permanent Committee Concerning Sovereignty and Defense* under the auspices of ALBA's Political Council. The goal of this body was to propose an integrated defense strategy and a school for military training and professional development. From the outset, the intent of the initiative was clear; to counter the perceived influence of the U.S. military in Latin America.

The school itself is located at Santa Rosa del Paquio in the town of Warnes, approximately thirteen kilometers from the commercial city of Santa Cruz de la Sierra, Bolivia. The facility spans 5,500 square meters and has the capacity to garrison over two hundred students at one time. It is believed that approximately $1.8 million dollars of seed funds were provided by Iran toward the school's construction and inauguration.

Although it is primarily a military facility, the school was also designed to be a training center for civilian leaders and defense officials from ALBA nations. This enhancement of civil-military relations is one of the school's core purposes, an attempt to "shape civilian and military leadership that will define the role of the armed forces for the study of defense, security and development in Latin America." There are no strict academic requirements for admission to the school, enabling civilian and military leaders from a wide range of academic levels to apply. A joint committee of representatives from each ALBA nation determines selection, with preference given to any individuals actively involved in current ALBA projects and reforms.

The curriculum of the school is atypical for a military training center. Military officers go through political instruction, while civilian officials are trained in military strategy. Foreign internal defense is a core component of the curriculum. When comparing this type of curriculum to other Latin American defense programs, the ALBA regional defense school rejects classification as a conventional military training facility. Rather, the school's content and objectives are more aligned with the tenets of asymmetric fourth-generation warfare.

To date, the ALBA regional defense school remains on "standby." Ironically, during its inauguration, the school was co-located with the U.S.-funded Bolivian Center for Peacekeeping Training (COMPEBOL), which has subsequently been relocated. In its place, a Bolivian Anti Aircraft Artillery unit, the "Felix Aguirre," currently occupies part of the facility and is nicknamed the "bodyguards" of the ALBA regional defense school.

All of the necessary infrastructure, in other words, is present. What has been absent so far has been the crucial order and resources from ALBA's leadership authorizing the school to become fully operational.

A SHARED ASYMMETRIC STRATEGY

Bolivia is a nation of limited military resources. The country's entire armed forces consist of no more than forty thousand soldiers,[3] with technology and conventional weapons systems that are insignificant, outdated and poorly maintained. In a conventional war, Bolivia's chances of victory would be slim. This prompts perplexing and important questions: Why would ALBA build a regional defense school in Bolivia? What role can Bolivia play in a regional security context? What type of confrontation is Bolivia preparing for, and how would it leverage its conventional military weakness against superior technology and strength?

Answering these questions requires a realization that Bolivia's current military weakness can be converted into strength in an alternative form of warfare, one that is unconventional and asymmetric.

Bolivia's conventional military weakness defines ALBA writ large. Should ALBA engage in a conventional war with its adversaries, its options would be limited. That said, in an unconventional asymmetric war, the conventional center of gravity shifts to favor the "weaker" countries, and political leadership and public opinion would lend ALBA the upper hand. The asymmetry of forces would justify the use of attacks via direct and indirect methods—both lethal and non-lethal—while encouraging active participation by the civilian population and non-state actors.[4] This idea is clearly an integral part of ALBA's security and defense doctrine and will be critical to the new joint military training that ALBA is pursuing among its member states.

Venezuela has already incorporated this form of unconventional warfare into its own military doctrine. The National Armed Forces of Venezuela (FAN, in its Spanish acronym) purchased thirty thousand copies of a military handbook version of Spanish ideologue Jorge Verstrynge's *Peripheral Warfare and Revolutionary Islam*.[5] The books were distributed among generals, chiefs of staff, and other Venezuelan flagship officers, as well as to a select group of government employees from different departments.[6] This new military doctrine of asymmetric warfare has been complemented by the creation and legalization of civilian "Bolivarian" militias, known colloquially as *colectivos*. Socialist ideology and the protection of political changes justify the doctrine, since civilians and other non-state actors are necessary for the asymmetric defense for Venezuela. These *colectivos* are a critical component of the Venezuelan government's response to grassroots protests in the spring of 2014, with violent and deadly results.

In Bolivia, the process of assimilating civilians into security and defense initiatives has advanced more slowly. Toward the end of 2006, a group of 120 soldiers, upon completion of their mandatory military service, were recruited for a pilot training program focused on counterterrorism, personal security, arms and explosives, communications, and first-aid. The pilot program was held at the Bolivian School of the Condors,[7] a prestigious military academy. Once the course was completed, the young soldiers were temporarily housed at a military barracks in La Paz, waiting to be deployed to Venezuela at a later date. Many of the civilians in the pilot program were supposedly trained under the pretext that they would serve on the presidential security team, but many believe them to be the initial formation of a Bolivian paramilitary force trained by Venezuela and Cuba.

Iran has the requisite knowledge to assist in this effort, because training civilian militias has been a core feature of the Islamic Republic since its founding in 1979. In response to the call for a "twenty million man army" at the start of the Islamic Revolution, Iran's revolutionaries created the *Basij*, a "people's" militia designed to help preserve social order. The *Basij* Resistance Force is a volunteer paramilitary organization that operates as an auxiliary force under the Iranian Revolutionary Guard Corps, with a presence in virtually every city and town in Iran. Today, the *Basij* is believed to have millions of members, and the militia was instrumental in suppressing dissent during the 2009 "Green Revolution" that followed the re-election of Mahmoud Ahmadinejad to the Iranian presidency. Notably, the *Basij* has also served as a model for other Middle Eastern civilian militias, most directly the *Shabiha* of Syria, which is currently aiding the Syrian government in its assault on opposition forces.

In April 2009, the current commander of the *Basij*, Brigadier General Mohammad Reza Naqdi, accompanied then-Iranian Defense Minister Mostafa Mohammad-Najjar on a high-level visit to Caracas at the invitation of the late President Hugo Chávez. A few years later, the purpose of this visit was laid bare when leaked government documents discussed Chavista plans to stir up civil unrest if Chávez were to lose the 2012 presidential election in Venezuela. The tactical playbook of the plan, including setting alphanumeric short codes and infiltrating universities, was strikingly similar to tactics used by the *Basij* against its own opposition. General Naqdi is also rumored to have visited Bolivia in May 2011, alongside former Iranian defense minister Ahmad Vahidi.

A GROWING DIPLOMATIC AND MILITARY PRESENCE

For its part, ALBA has encouraged the inclusion of Iran (together with Syria) as an observer state in its political bloc. In turn, the organization has become one of Iran's most important strategic allies. And with the exception of Venezuela, Bolivia is Iran's most important ally within the bloc, as evidenced by the size of its diplomatic presence in the country, as well as the scope of its military cooperation with the Islamic Republic.

That cooperation is now extensive and far-reaching, based upon a framework agreement signed in September 2007, following Iranian President Mahmoud Ahmadinejad's first official visit to Bolivia. Rhetorically, the framework established the precedent for future collaborative projects in order to encourage "world peace and sustainable development around the world." In practice, it served as the start of a bilateral relationship between two nations without much in common.

Although the agreement was signed in 2007, it was not submitted to Bolivia's Congress until April of 2010.[8] At the time of the signing, the Morales regime had not yet consolidated its control over the legislature. Thus, the framework faced significant political opposition when Morales initially tried to gain approval for an increased Iranian presence in the country. The Bolivian Senate, in particular, raised many concerns regarding the underlying purpose of the newfound relationship. But three years later, in June 2010, Evo Morales' Movement Towards Socialism (MAS) political party gained the two-thirds majority necessary for congressional ratification. The 2007 bilateral accord between Iran and Bolivia has since been easily ratified and approved.

Cooperation, however, preceded formal approval by Bolivia's parliament. In February 2008, the Islamic Republic opened its first embassy in La Paz. In turn, President Morales announced that Bolivia would relocate its Middle Eastern embassy from Cairo to Tehran. From that point on, diplomatic engagement accelerated rapidly. In July 2009, Masoud Edrisi, the Iranian business attaché in La Paz, announced that the Iranian mission in Bolivia had just three diplomats in residence. Only three years later, that number had ballooned to at least 145—showcasing the rapid expansion of political contacts.[9]

The large Iranian presence in Bolivia raises several questions:

1. Does the Iranian Embassy in Bolivia have the capacity to absorb so many working officials in such a small country?
2. Where in Bolivia are all of these Iranian officials working, and what kind of work are they performing?
3. If there are 145 credentialed Iranian diplomats in country, how many more are non-credentialed—and how many belong to the feared Revolutionary Guard Corps?

These questions remain unanswered. Nevertheless, they are an important part of Iran's changing presence in Latin America.

In the wake of the diplomatic incident triggered by Vahidi's arrival in Warnes, Iran has been forced to seek other justifications for its strategic presence in Bolivia. This has led to a more recent bilateral agreement between the two countries, signed on June 20, 2012, and purportedly intended to combat drug trafficking. That pretext, however, is questionable, not least because several high-level Morales cabinet officials have been criminally implicated in drug scandals, most notably the former drug czar, René Sanabria, and the current Minister of the Presidency, Juan Ramon Quintana. Thus, if Iran was actually intending to join the crusade against Latin American drug trafficking, Bolivia would hardly be considered its first choice as partner.

However, the recent counternarcotics accord establishes the precedent for a robust Iranian military presence in Bolivia. It contains a confidential clause allowing Iran to train and advise Bolivian armed forces engaged in anti-drug trafficking operations. Application of this agreement will mostly take place in a remote sub-region frequently recognized as the epicenter of transnational organized crime in South America: Chapare.

CLANDESTINE COOPERATION IN CHAPARE

Slightly larger than 1 million square kilometers in size, Bolivia is territorially the fourth largest country in the region. It shares 6,750 kilometers of borders with Brazil, Paraguay, Argentina, Chile, and Peru. Its location in the center of South America provides an axis point for transit north to south and east to west, connecting both the Pacific Ocean to the Atlantic and the Amazon basin to the Andean ridge. However, there are indisputable downsides to Bolivia's geographic position. Bolivia's densely populated areas are quite small relative to the size of the territory; on average, there are approximately seven inhabitants per square kilometer in the country. Furthermore, aside from the Lake Titicaca region in the west and a handful of other small settler groups, vast expanses of the country are virtually uninhabited. As a result, the Bolivian government lacks a robust presence in many parts of its own territory.

Moreover, a privileged geographic location and rich concentration of natural resources[10] do not automatically translate into prosperity and economic development.[11] According to some estimates, some 70 percent of the Bolivian population lives in extreme or moderate poverty. Predictably, therefore, contraband smuggling and illegal narcotics play a dominant role in the Bolivian informal economy, and in society as a whole. This state of affairs is coupled with high-levels of (often government-sanctioned) corruption in the public sphere, and exacerbated by the inefficiency and ineffectiveness of state public institutions.

The heartland region of Chapare exemplifies all of these failings. It functions under the complete political, social, and military control of the Coca Grower's Union—affectionately nicknamed the *Cocaleros*—and every public institution and local government leader is beholden to Evo Morales, who has served as the leader of the *Cocaleros* since 1996. The Bolivian police and military units operating in Chapare are also loyal to the regime and its professed ideology. Over the course of Morales' term in office, he has invested state resources heavily in the development of Chapare, funding an agroindustrial park, a petrochemical plant, and what will soon be Bolivia's largest international airport. But no initiative has been more controversial than the construction of a paved road through the Isiboro Sécure National Park (TIPNIS) for the expansion of coca leaf plantations. The TIPNIS initiative has provoked anger from many indigenous groups, who assert that Morales is only paving this road to expand illegal drug production. [12]

The command and control structure the *Cocaleros*, their connection to organized crime, their radical ideology and support from the government, has led some analysts to compare them to the Taliban in Afghanistan—insinuating that they have the composition of a future insurgency in Bolivia.

Iranian assistance to anti-narcotic efforts in Bolivia would likely take place in Chapare. If successful, the effort would effectively place Iranian military "advisors" in one of the most conflict-ridden zones in South America under the complete protection of the politically popular *Cocaleros*. Such conditions are ideal for Iranian covert activity in Bolivia, because the national government, the *Cocaleros*, and President Morales himself will provide any necessary plausible deniability.

DANGEROUS CONSEQUENCES

On June 14, 2014, Iran's vice president, Es'haq Jahangiri, touched down in Santa Cruz, Bolivia, to take part in the 50th anniversary of the G77 + China Extraordinary Summit. Hassan Rouhani, Iran's new president, was initially slated to take part in the summit, but the vice president was sent as a last minute replacement. As the host of the summit, Morales laid out the red carpet for Jahangiri and the Iranian delegation, which resulted in a $200 million credit line being extended to Bolivia by the Islamic Republic. [13]

Political solidarity and sustainable development were the major topics of discussions on the floor of the summit in Santa Cruz. However, on the sidelines more controversial conversations took place. [14] For the last couple of years, Bolivia has joined Iran in the pursuit of nuclear power. Aided by Argentina (one of only two countries in Latin America with nuclear technology), Bolivia has begun preliminary work on building its first nuclear reactor through a new high-level energy commission and sending several physicists and nuclear engineers for training at the Bariloche Atomic Centre run by Argentina's National Atomic Energy Commission (CNEA). Given the close relationship between Bolivia and Iran, and the latter's encroachment toward Argentina—future bilateral nuclear cooperation does not seem an implausible scenario. [15]

ALBA's new security and defense initiatives will have far reaching effects—for Bolivia, for the region, and for Iran's place in it. The ALBA regional defense school represents a new framework for a potential mass paramilitary presence across the continent. Moreover, Bolivia's Chapare region can serve as the epicenter for clandestine activities in the heart of South America. This has been coupled with, and augmented by, the intrusion of Iranian military and paramilitary officers into Bolivia.

The true objectives of the extensive Iranian presence in Bolivia are not transparent. What we do know, however, is that Bolivia has become a base for Iran's asymmetric activities in South America, a point that has largely been lost on regional security scholars.

NOTES

1. Alejandro Peña Esclusa, *El Foro de Sao Paulo. Una amenaza continental* [The Foro of Sao Paolo. A Continental Threat] (Bogotá: Grijalbo, 2010).

2. "Evo y Chávez proponen crear Consejo de Defensa Militar de Alba," [Evo and Chávez Propose the Creation of an ALBA Military Defense Council] Opinion.com.bo, February 5, 2012, http://www.opinion.com.bo/opinion/articulos/2012/0205/noticias.php?id=42582.

3. Bolivia mandates military service for its citizens, and thus, an average of thirty-four thousand new recruits serve each year. Additionally, there are approximately six thousand members of the Bolivian armed forces (between officers and non-commissioned officers).

4. In June 2007, Bolivian president Evo Morales indicated that the armed forces are part of the "change process." He also pointed out that the military institution is not only vital for Bolivia but also for the region. He stated that future stances would not come from the government but instead from the social movements. See http://www.alianzabolivariana.org/modules. php?name=Newsandfile=articleandsid=1970. That very same month, Venezuelan President Hugo Chávez indicated that the Venezuelan armed forces ought to apply a new military mentality more aligned with the current world reality and the new global war declared by United States. This should be an asymmetric war in which Venezuela has fully engaged. See http:// www.alianzabolivariana.org/modules.php?name=Newsandfile=articleandsid=2045.

5. Héctor Herrera Jiménez, a Venezuelan military officer, pointed out in September of 2008 that traditional war between nations, with delimited borders or armies in uniform along with flags and national anthems, will decrease in frequency, and that societies will more likely be attacked using a combination of ideas, technology, media, and traditional wartime actions. See http://www.alianzabolivariana.org/modules.php?name=Newsandfile=articleandsid=2866.

6. Antonio Salas, *El Palestino* [The Palestinian] (Buenos Aires: Editorial Planeta, 2010).

7. Located in the Department (State) of Tarija, in Bolivia, it is considered one of the best centers for military formation in Latin America, with a high level of academic achievement and solid international reputation among its elite military officers.

8. The start of diplomatic relations in 2007 was heralded by important announcements of Iranian investments in Bolivia with an estimated value of $1.1 billion. The cooperation framework was to be carried out in five years. The five years passed, and yet the offer remains mostly conceptual. While the differences between initial expectations and results are large, Iran's influence is nevertheless undeniable. In February 2009, Iran granted Bolivia a loan of $280 million. The loan was the largest since the beginning of the bilateral relationship. These resources were distributed without specific caveats for allocation.

9. Jorge Marirrodriga, "Irán se lanza a la conquista de Latinoamérica," [Iran Launches the Conquest of Latin America] *El Pais* (Madrid), June 23, 2012, http://internacional.elpais.com/ internacional/2012/06/23/actualidad/1340465739_921466.html.

10. Bolivia has the fourth largest forest in South America. In the region, it ranks fourth in terms of arable land and water reservation; fifth in terms of gas; and first in terms of iron reserves. Furthermore, Bolivia has the largest global reserve of lithium and exports the greatest quantities of zinc and silver. It also has significant reserves of uranium and other rare minerals. Most of its resources are located in the southeast part of the country, whereas the country's larger population concentrations are in the west.

11. In countries like Bolivia, whose economies are entirely dependent on the exploitation of natural resources, these resources define a complex and defined web of social relations.

12. The indigenous peoples living in the TIPNIS area marched to the seat of government in 2011 and 2012 to protest the construction of this road since they, reasonably, fear the invasion of coca growers in their territories. This kind of protest also occurred years ago in Chapare when a road to connect the cities of Santa Cruz de la Sierra and Cochabamba was built. In that instance, the indigenous groups were dispersed to the territories they now occupy. Further validating their fears is the fact that these coca growers/settlers are already present in the southern area of the park and they are illegally growing coca leaves and defending the project to construct the road project.

13. Tehran Times, "Iranian VP Meets Bolivian, Zimbabwean Presidents," Political Desk, June 15, 2014, http://www.tehrantimes.com/politics/116306-iranian-vp-meets-bolivian-zimbab wean-presidents-.

14. Notishots, "Claves Secretas de la Cumbre G77" *Eju.tv* (Santa Cruz), June 16, 2014, http://eju.tv/2014/06/claves-secretas-de-la-cumbre-g77/.

15. For a detailed discussion on nuclear cooperation and capabilities in Latin America, see: Fernando Menéndez, "A Nuclear Latin America?" Issue 9, Defense Dossier of the American Foreign Policy Council, December 2013, http://www.afpc.org/files/december2013.pdf.

Chapter Nine

Rewriting History in Argentina

Julian M. Obiglio and Diego C. Naveira

In 1994, Argentina suffered one of the largest terrorist attacks ever to take place in the Western Hemisphere. On July 18 of that year, the *Asociación Mutual Israelita Argentina* (AMIA), a Jewish cultural center in Buenos Aires, was brutally bombed, killing 85 people and injuring hundreds more. The AMIA attack followed a previous, smaller one that had taken place on the Israeli embassy in 1992, killing another 29 people and formally introducing Argentina to the murky world of international Islamic terrorism.

The investigations that immediately followed the AMIA attack were riddled with incompetence and accusations of cover-ups. This led to the impeachment of a federal judge and the mishandling of evidence that further complicated the case. For more than a decade, Argentine authorities did not advance the AMIA case—until then-President Néstor Kirchner lifted a decree in 2003 that prevented Argentine authorities from testifying. This prompted another investigation by prosecutors Alberto Nisman and Marcelo Martínez Burgos who, on October 25, 2006, announced their conclusion that the attack was "ordered by the highest authorities of the Islamic Republic of Iran in conjunction with Hezbollah."[1]

Argentina has since sought the extradition of six high-ranking Iranian officials linked to the bombing, and has ordered the arrest of two others. However, the Argentine government's failure to capture, try, and convict the bombing suspects to date highlights the incoherent policy toward Iran that prevailed in the years following the attacks, culminating in a controversial 2013 memorandum signed by the leaders of both countries to reinvestigate the bombings for which the perpetrators had already been indicted.

How did this happen? Once counted among the top countries in the world in terms of GDP, Argentina has become increasingly dependent on alternative sources of trade in recent years as the current president, Cristina

Fernández de Kirchner, leads the country deeper and deeper into financial ruin and international isolation. Relations with formerly friendly Western powers such as the United States and Spain are growing increasingly antagonistic, while the Fernández de Kirchner administration seeks warmer diplomatic ties with other populist Latin American governments, namely Venezuela and Cuba. Indeed, Venezuela's former president, the late Hugo Chávez, is known to have exerted an inordinate amount of influence on Fernández de Kirchner, aiding the reopening of relations with Iran and thereby allowing the Islamic Republic to regain lost ground in Argentina.

A DANGEROUS FLIRTATION

While Argentina and Iran maintained less-than-friendly diplomatic relations following the 1994 attacks, Argentine UN Ambassador Jorge Arguello signaled a thaw in the two countries' relations during the 2011 General Assembly. Rather than walking out, as had been Argentina's tradition until then, Arguello remained seated during the Iranian president's address in New York.[2] Moreover, in recent years, Argentina seems to have put aside its contentious past with Iran in favor of establishing a new political ally and source of economic support, something it desperately needs at this juncture.

President Fernández de Kirchner's populist economic policies, including: massive public spending, increased regulation, higher taxes, trade barriers, and poor monetary policy have led to chaos, a dwindling economic growth rate, high levels of inflation and unemployment, and a drop in foreign reserves that have thrown Argentina into economic free fall. As depicted in Figure 9.1, the country's reserves dropped more than $20 billion in just a few years, plummeting from $52 billion in 2010 to $30 billion towards the end of 2013. This has led to a wide disparity between the official exchange rate (pegged at approximately 7 pesos to the dollar), and the unofficial rate, which is closer to 12 pesos per dollar, thereby creating an informal market known locally as the *dolár blue*.[3]

This economic tailspin has spawned a dangerous government response. Strapped for cash, Fernández de Kirchner sponsored a new law in March of 2013 that allows any amount of funds from anywhere in the world to be invested in Argentina, essentially inviting international money launderers to put their dollars in Argentine banks.[4] And, increasingly isolated from traditional Western allies, Fernández de Kirchner has sought alternative trade alliances with non-aligned countries, particularly Iran and Venezuela.

Argentina's desperate need for dollars has been compounded by a deep dependence on oil and gas, which make up 90 percent of the country's primary energy sources. During the last decade, both Kirchner administrations changed the role of Argentina's energy sector, increasing taxes on oil

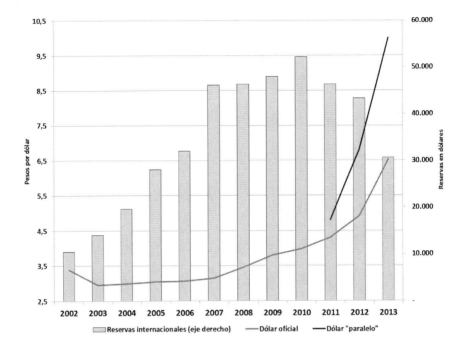

Figure 9.1. **Official vs. unofficial exchange rate vis-à-vis foreign reserves (in USD) data taken from figures at Central Bank of the Republic of Argentina**

exports, setting price controls on hydrocarbons and ultimately driving away foreign investment, leading to a dramatic decrease in energy production. This created disequilibrium between the supply and demand of energy, and Argentina began to import more than it exports—something that had not happened in more than twenty years, as depicted in Figure 9.2.

This state of affairs has only added incentive for the Argentine government to reverse its policy toward Iran.

The results have been notable. In 2012, media reports began covering Argentina's new "transactional" foreign policy, in which Buenos Aires bartered away its international position in return for dividends received from the Islamic Republic.[5] In September of that year, Foreign Minister Hector Timmerman met with his then-Iranian counterpart, Ali Akbar Salehi, at the UN General Assembly in New York to initiate formal discussions related to the AMIA bombings of 1994. President Fernández de Kirchner's public announcement of these discussions gave the impression that this was a sudden shift in Argentina's international position regarding Iran. In reality, however, Timmerman had been meeting with Salehi behind closed doors as far back as January 2011, when he traveled to Aleppo, Syria, to initiate discussions with

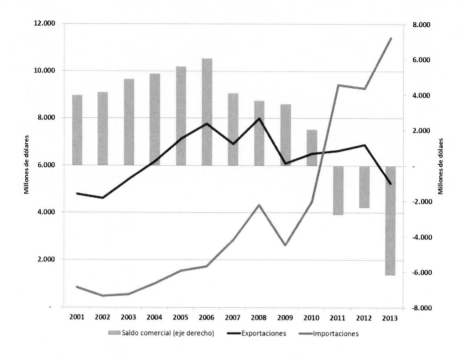

Figure 9.2. **Energy imports vs. exports vis-à-vis commercial exchange (in millions USD) data taken from INDEC database**

Iran.[6] Syrian President Bashar al-Assad and his Foreign Minister, Walid al-Moallem, are known to have mediated the talks.[7] The visit prompted Iran to publicly declare that they are interested in knowing "the truth" behind the AMIA bombing, perhaps because they now felt secure that Argentina would no longer be pursuing serious investigations against their officials.

The effort is logical. If Iran can manage to adjudicate the Buenos Aires bombings in its favor, absolving itself of all responsibility and increasing its international legitimacy as a result, an enhanced financial relationship between the two countries may follow. In turn, a potential Iranian "stimulus" would provide much needed support for Fernández de Kirchner's rapidly deteriorating reputation and economy.

But the rapprochement taking place between Argentina and Iran goes beyond AMIA. In recent years, bilateral trade and political cooperation has continued to grow, despite objections from the influential Jewish community and other opposition groups in Argentina. Since President Fernández de Kirchner took office in 2003, Argentine exports to Iran have risen from $319 million to a little over $1 billion, and the country has become one of Iran's principal food suppliers (principally in beef, soybeans, and wheat).[8]

Financial and energy support from Iran is likely a major force behind Argentina's change of attitude toward the Islamic Republic. However, the thaw did not happen without some salesmanship from Hugo Chávez.

CHÁVEZ'S ROLE

Venezuela's late president played an outsized role in facilitating Iran's renewed relationship with Argentina. By offering preferential oil deals and direct cash payments, Chávez successfully seduced many Latin American governments to join his "Bolivarian" revolution. Argentina's energy deficit and debt nudged the Fernández de Kirchner regime closer towards Venezuela's petro-diplomacy and, by extension, toward Venezuela's top Mideast ally, Iran.[9]

Chávez's courtship of Fernández de Kirchner was an ongoing effort. The Washington, D.C.-based American Enterprise Institute reported in July of 2011 that the former president of Iran, Mahmud Ahmadinejad, had allegedly asked Chávez to reach out to Fernández de Kirchner through diplomatic channels in 2007 in order to "change Argentine policy and allow Iran access to Argentina's nuclear technology."[10] Subsequently, Venezuela made several suspicious payments to Argentina, authorizing a number of commercial ventures to be carried out in collaboration with Iran in the rural Argentine province of Sante Fe, near the Rio Parana River. This area happens to be a port of entry for a known drug smuggling route between Argentina to Venezuela.[11]

Before he passed away from cancer in April 2013, Chávez had remained silent about Argentina and Iran's most recent diplomatic ventures. But behind the scenes, the Venezuelan leader established an informal line of communication between Tehran, Caracas, and the *Casa Rosada* (presidential palace) of Cristina Fernández de Kirchner. The nexus of this communication was a Chilean journalist, Paula Chahin Ananías, employed in the press secretary's office of the Fernández de Kirchner administration. Chahin resides in Argentina as a result of the political exile of her husband, former Chilean guerilla leader Galvarino Apablaza Guerra, who is accused of having assassinated Chilean Senator Jaime Guzman.[12]

The 1991 assassination of Guzman, who played an important role in drafting the most recent Chilean constitution, is an important landmark in Chilean history. Argentina's unwillingness to extradite Apablaza runs the risk of igniting a diplomatic spat between the two countries, particularly if Chilean officials determine that Fernández de Kirchner is knowingly harboring this terrorist.[13]

Chávez capitalized on this state of affairs by sending one of his top diplomats with ties to the Middle East to reach out to Chahin—and through her to Fernández de Kirchner. The objective was to persuade the Argentine president to reconsider her government's political posture toward Iran, and Paula Chahin was offered protection and potential asylum for her exiled husband as an incentive. [14]

The ploy worked. Under Chávez's influence, Fernández de Kirchner and Iran bridged the gap created by the 1994 AMIA attacks to create a new, seemingly symbiotic relationship. The lion's share of the benefits from this newfound relationship are reaped by Iran, because an alliance with Argentina increases trade opportunities with countries in the Western Hemisphere, strengthens its political image against allegations of human rights violations, and provides the perfect setting for the Islamic Republic to expand and strengthen its proxy terrorist network in Latin America. Meanwhile, Argentina continues to suffer economically and politically under the watchful gaze of its new "allies."

Venezuela's role in the Argentine political scene has diminished since Chávez's death. Internal turmoil has prevented the current Venezuelan president, Nicolás Maduro, from pursuing his predecessor's priorities of aggressive regional influence, at least for the moment. But signs of Venezuela's activity in Argentina still remain.

Only two weeks before Chávez's death, Argentina reached an agreement to transfer medium-range missile technology to Venezuela's *Compañía Anónima Venezolana de Industrias Militares* (CAVIM), a public arms firm currently sanctioned by the U.S. Department of Treasury for its ties to Tehran. [15] Venezuela's influence can also be seen in the purchase of fuel from PDVSA, Venezuela's state-owned oil and natural gas company, to feed Argentina's expanding energy deficit (and grow its public debt in the process).

A CONTROVERSY OVER THE "TRUTH"

On January 27, 2013, Iran signed a Memorandum of Understanding (MOU) with Argentina to reinvestigate the circumstances of the 1994 AMIA attack. The agreement was signed in Ethiopia between Iran's then-former foreign minister, Ali Akbar Salehi, and his Argentine counterpart, Hector Timerman. Among the provisions of the agreement was the establishment of a Truth Commission, made up of five international jurists, who would analyze all of the documentation presented in the case by both countries and provide recommendations for making progress in the investigation.

Since then, however, the joint agreement has run into considerable difficulty. Resistant to many of Argentina's requests, Iran refused to cooperate with numerous provisions of the MOU, and appeared reluctant to contribute information related to the case to the investigation. A particular bone of contention was its refusal to allow Iranian officials implicated in the AMIA attack to be questioned. Instead, Iran provided contradictory reports regarding their disposition and openly condemned INTERPOL "red notices" issued against these officials, two of whom (Mohsen Razai and Ali Akbar Velayati) were candidates in the 2013 Iranian presidential elections.[16]

By May of 2013, five months after the accord was signed, Argentine Foreign Minister Héctor Timerman released an official statement that his office still had not received a formal notification of Iran's approval of the agreement. It was not until almost a year after the original introduction of the agreement that Iran gave its formal approval for it.[17] Yet despite these red flags, Argentina continues to pursue and strengthen diplomatic ties with the Islamic Republic, regardless high-level Iranian officials are accused of planning and implementing the 1994 attack.

The identities of those individuals provide some insights into why Iran is so interested in their protection. Tellingly, chief among those implicated in the AMIA attacks are former Iranian Defense Minister General Ahmad Vahidi and Mohsen Rabbani, Iran's former Cultural Attaché to Argentina (and the godfather of Iranian influence in Latin America).

Vahidi made a controversial visit to Latin America in May of 2011 to inaugurate the regional defense school for the Bolivarian Alliance of the Americas (ALBA) in Warnes, Bolivia. An existing INTERPOL red notice and criticism from the Jewish community in Buenos Aires forced him to cut his trip short and beat a hasty retreat back to Iran, using diplomatic immunity to avoid extradition to Argentina.[18]

The purported mastermind of the AMIA attack, however, is Iranian cleric Mohsen Rabbani. Usually quiet and secretive, Rabbani broke his silence in an interview with the Brazilian daily *Folha de Sao Paulo* on October 21, 2012, mere months before the joint agreement between Iran and Argentina was announced. In the interview, Rabbani proclaimed his innocence, disavowed any association with the Iranian regime and mentioned that his last visit to the region was to Brazil in 1998.[19]

The facts, however, suggest otherwise. According to Argentine special prosecutor Alberto Nisman, Rabbani is an agent of Iran's Ministry of Intelligence and Security (MOIS) and has visited the region many times since fleeing Argentina. Moreover, Rabbani maintains his presence in Latin America through an array of disciples he has developed in Latin America over decades, with one of his original emissaries being none other than Guyanese parliamentarian Abdul Kadir, a recruited agent of Iran who was convicted as one of the plotters of the failed 2007 plot to bomb New York's JFK international airport.[20]

According to a 500-page indictment released by Nisman in May of 2013, Kadir was trained and supported by Iran, and maintained a close relationship with Rabbani. Based in Guyana, Kadir established an intelligence structure remarkably similar to the one that had been built by Rabbani in Buenos Aires prior to the AMIA attacks, where "propaganda about Islam was made and they tried to convert people so that they would join the Shia movement in Guyana."[21] Investigation into Kadir's role in Iran's terrorist network shows that these intelligence structures all have a single and unique leadership, implying that they are preconceived plans that form part of a larger end goal (the exportation of the Islamic revolution), and whose structures link them inextricably to the Iranian government.

Operations such as the one Abdul Kadir managed in Guyana highlight Iran's tactical playbook for infiltration and indoctrination in the Western Hemisphere. Iranian embassies use diplomatic representations and cultural, religious, and charity associations to conceal their intelligence activities. Moreover, embassies empower these activities with diplomatic immunity, backdoor channels, and access to local governments. Various Islamic communities throughout the Americas are a principal target of these operations, and are penetrated by mosques and Islamic charities that serve as intelligence collection centers (or, as Nisman calls them, "antennas" of the Iranian revolution).

The two most prominent Rabbani disciples active in Argentina and neighboring countries are Edgardo Ruben "Suhail" Assad and his brother-in-law Santiago Paz Bullrich, a.k.a. Abdul Karim Paz. Together these "sheiks" serve as Iran's informal ambassadors in Latin America and travel throughout the region unifying and radicalizing Islamic communities as they recruit, proselytize and indoctrinate young Latin Americans into radical Islam. [22]

Today there are believed to be more than 40 Islamic organizations linked to Rabbani's extensive network throughout Latin America.[23] And many of the indigenous militant Islamic leaders that have emerged on the scene in recent years in South America have done so thanks to the "blind eye" of Argentine authorities. These Islamists are all disciples of the "terrorist professor," Mohsen Rabbani, who planted the intellectual seeds for their radicalism back in the 1980s and is now reaping the rewards in the form of cultural centers and mosques spreading from Tierra del Fuego to the Rio Grande. Meanwhile, the Fernández de Kirchner regime has—either intentionally or unintentionally—emboldened this network by seeking closer relations with the ayatollahs in Tehran.

ONE STEP FORWARD, TWO STEPS BACK

President Fernández de Kirchner originally defended the agreement with Iran against widespread opposition, saying that the most important thing was to "act in good faith, with responsibility, with no opportunism and with commitment to truth, memory, and justice" in investigating the AMIA attacks.[24] She insisted that the agreement did not have geopolitical underpinnings, and her dialogue with Iran was an honest effort to discover the truth about the

1994 bombing. Iran parroted her rhetoric, saying that the main goal in the investigation was to discover the truth: nothing more, nothing less.

Less than a year later, however, Argentina would send mixed signals regarding its stance toward Iran by voting against it at the United Nations Human Rights Council in a measure supporting continued monitoring of Iran's abuses of human rights.[25] Then, in March of 2014, in a formal address before the nation, Argentina's President explicitly stated that she would abrogate the accord with Iran due to lack of progress and growing internal opposition: "As president, I pledge to terminate this agreement [with Iran] and carry out what they propose. Memory, truth, and justice should not be just a slogan."[26]

Discussions between Iran and Argentina regarding the agreement stalled late last year, and Fernández de Kirchner and Timerman met with AMIA to discuss the preparation of an alternative plan to investigate the 1994 case.[27] At that point, it seemed that she was beginning to distance herself from Iran and Venezuela—whose regimes were preoccupied with internal politics— and seeking to minimize the fallout of what had turned into an embarrassment for Argentina.

The reversal was prompted by the work of Argentina's Jewish community, which—along with state prosecutor Alberto Nisman—requested that the judge in charge of the AMIA case declare the Argentina-Iran agreement unconstitutional. Their argument was based on the fact that the memorandum, which establishes an international political body, moves the case from the Argentine judicial system into the hands of the executive. Nisman further argued that this violates the Republican form of government in Argentina (namely the division of powers) since it would give the national executive authority over a case that belongs to the judiciary.

But the pendulum has begun to swing back once again. The Argentine government recently initiated an appeal before the very court that had declared the memorandum unconstitutional. As a result, what appeared to be an easy "out" for the Fernández de Kirchner regime has turned into continued controversy and still more political posturing.

Whether Argentina will break, or at least loosen, ties with Iran remains to be seen. But it is safe to say that Cristina Fernández de Kirchner places a priority on her reputation and prefers to avoid looking weak before the nation or the international community, even at the expense of consistency in her foreign policy decisions. She thus prefers to terminate the accord on her terms, and will not tolerate letting it fall into the hands of the country's judiciary. Meanwhile, the victims of the AMIA bombing continue to endure this political circus, while Argentinians at large suffer the disastrous effects of the Argentine government's decisions.

NOTES

Rachel Echeto from the University of Southern California contributed to this chapter.

1. Marcelo Martinez Burgos and Alberto Nisman, "AMIA Case," Investigations Unit of the Office of the Attorney General, 2006, http://www.peaceandtolerance.org/docs/nismanindict.pdf.

2. Carolina Barros, "Argentina Hears Out Iran," *Buenos Aires Herald*, September 23, 2011, http://www.buenosairesherald.com/article/79644/argentina-hears-out-iran.

3. Ken Parks, "Argentina's Peso Hits Record Lows on Black Market," *Wall Street Journal*, January 15, 2014, http://online.wsj.com/news/articles/SB10001424052702304603704579322750262415232.

4. Douglas Farah, "Cristinanomics," *Foreign Policy*, June 4, 2013, http://www.foreignpolicy.com/articles/2013/06/04/cristina_fernandez_argentina_money_laundering.

5. Ilan Berman, "The Dangerous Iran Flirtation," *Washington Times*, September 27, 2012, http://www.washingtontimes.com/news/2012/sep/27/at-first-blush-argentina-seems-like-an-odd-choice-/.

6. Pepe Eliaschev, "El Gobierno negocia un pacto secreto con Irán para 'olvidar' los atentados," Perfil.com, March 26, 2011, http://www.perfil.com/contenidos/2011/03/26/noticia_0004.html.

7. "Encuentro entre el Presidente de Siria Bashar Al-Assad y el Canciller argentino Hector Timerman," Prensa Islámica, January 24, 2011, http://www.prensaislamica.com/nota6310.html.

8. Douglas Farah, *Back to the Future: Argentina Unravels* (Inter-American Institute for Democracy, 2013), 75.

9. Jaime Darenblum, *Has Argentina Joined the Chávez Bloc?* (Hudson Institute, 2011), http://www.hudson.org/content/researchattachments/attachment/870/argentinafinal.pdf.

10. Roger Noriega, "Argentina's Secret Deal with Iran?" American Enterprise Institute, July 2011, http://www.aei-ideas.org/2011/07/argentinas-secret-deal-with-iran/.

11. Eugenio Burzaco, "Las vias que nos llevan a ser un pais narco" *La Nacion* (Buenos Aires), November 6, 2013, http://www.lanacion.com.ar/1635764-las-vias-que-nos-llevan-a-ser-un-pais-narco.

12. "La Esposa de Apablaza y su estrecho," *El Mercurio* (Chile), September 26, 2010.

13. "Sigue la tension por Apablaza," Perfil.com, August 10, 2010, http://www.perfil.com/contenidos/2010/10/08/noticia_0006.html.

14. Author's interviews with confidential sources in Venezuela, March 2013.

15. Farah, *Back to the Future*, 61–62.

16. "Tehran Insists Accord with Argentina Includes Interpol Lifting Red Notices against Iranian Suspects," MercoPress, March 19, 2013, http://en.mercopress.com/2013/03/19/tehran-insists-accord-with-argentina-includes-interpol-lifting-red-notices-against-iranian-suspects.

17. "'No Formal Notification' about Iran's AMIA Deal Approval," *Buenos Aires Herald* May 21, 2013, http://www.buenosairesherald.com/article/131588/no-formal-notification-about-irans-amia-deal-approval.

18. Robin Yapp, "Iran Defence Minister Forced to Leave Bolivia over 1994 Argentina Bombing," *Telegraph* (London), June 1, 2011, http://www.telegraph.co.uk/news/worldnews/southamerica/bolivia/8550445/Iran-defence-minister-forced-to-leave-Bolivia-over-1994-Argentina-bombing.html.

19. Samy Adghirni, "Iranian Cleric Denies Participation in Attack in Argentina in 1994," *Folha de Sao Paulo*, October 23, 2012, http://www1.folha.uol.com.br/internacional/en/foreign/1173674-iranian-cleric-denies-participation-in-attack-in-argentina-in-1994.shtml.

20. Matthew Levitt, "Exporting Terror in America's Backyard," *Foreign Policy,* June 13, 2013, http://www.foreignpolicy.com/articles/2013/06/13/tehran_exporting_terror_latin_america.

21. The English-language translation of Alberto Nisman's recent indictment is available online at http://www.defenddemocracy.org/stuff/uploads/documents/summary_%2831_pages%29.pdf.

22. Joseph Humire, "Iran's Informal Ambassadors in Latin America," *Fox News Latino*, February 18, 2012, http://latino.foxnews.com/latino/politics/2012/02/18/joseph-humire-irans-informal-ambassadors-to-latin-america/.

23. Farah, *Back to the Future*, 77.

24. "AMIA Deal: 'The Most Important Thing Is to Act in Good Faith,' CFK Says," *Buenos Aires Herald*, March 15, 2013, http://www.buenosairesherald.com/article/126458/amia-deal-the-most-important-thing-is-to-act-in-good-faith-cfk-says (accessed June 30, 2014).

25. "Argentina Votes against Irán at UN Human Rights Council," *Buenos Aires Herald*, March 22, 2013, http://www.buenosairesherald.com/article/127012/argentina-votes-against-irán-at-un-human-rights-council.

26. "Argentina's President Says She Will Cancel Agreement with Iran on Jewish Center Attack," JTA, March 3, 2014, http://www.jta.org/2014/03/03/news-opinion/world/argentinas-president-says-she-will-cancel-agreement-with-iran-over-jewish-center-attack.

27. "Argentina Ready to Nix AMIA Truth Commission Pact with Iran," The Iran Project, March 4, 2014, http://theiranproject.com/blog/2014/03/04/argentina-ready-to-nix-amia-truth-commission-pact-with-iran/.

Chapter Ten

Anticipating Iran's Next Moves

Joseph M. Humire

After more than thirty years of engagement with the region, Iran has an astute understanding of the prevalent political patterns and socio-economic trends in Latin America. This is especially true after the last decade, during which Bolivarian countries (namely Venezuela and Bolivia) provided Iran with unparalleled access to the region. More recent years, however, have seen a period of stagnation for Iran's intrusion south of the border, as Latin America and the Islamic Republic each underwent significant political and economic changes. These shifts have led Iran to reassess its priorities, presence and activities in the region.

The Bolivarian alliance that once dominated the political scene in Latin America, and which is widely considered to have been Iran's gateway to the region, is changing. The loss of the bloc's charismatic leader, Hugo Chávez, to cancer in March of 2013, along with the subsequent collapse of Venezuela's petro-fueled economy, dealt a significant blow to Tehran.[1] Since then, no single political figure has emerged to carry on the "Bolivarian revolution," putting the long-term future of that political project in doubt. Adding to the uncertainty, more than half of the countries in the region have recently held presidential elections, or will do so between today and 2015—reshaping Latin America's political future in the process.

Throughout this transitional period, Iran has continually reassessed the region's political and economic environment, and prepared its next strategic moves accordingly. As a consequence, formal relations with several Latin American states have either remained static or diminished, with none as vibrant as they were in the previous decade. For example, whereas in 2008 trade with Venezuela had risen to approximately $80 million (primarily exports), 2013 saw only $19.4 million in bilateral commerce—a 75 percent drop in trade between Iran and one of its principal partners in the region.[2]

Nevertheless, in aggregate, the Islamic Republic maintains more influence than ever in the region. Yet it would also be fair to say that Iran's presence has reached an inflection point, one that requires careful assessment and analysis.

BACK TO BASICS

As Iran has gone back to the drawing board in Latin America, it naturally has sought strategic advice from its most fraternal ally there: Cuba. Historically, the Castro regime has relied heavily on external alliances, dating all the way back to the 1959 Cuban revolution. After all, it was Cuba's close alliance with the Soviet Union that brought the world to the brink of nuclear war during the 1962 Cuban Missile Crisis. Less well known is the Castro regime's relatively quiet relationship with the ayatollahs of Iran. In 1981, shortly after Iran's revolution, Cuba became the first country to officially recognize the new Islamic Republic by inviting it to open its first embassy in Latin America.[3] Since then, Cuba has been Iran's go-to ally in expanding its regional foreign policy portfolio.

It was predictable, then, that approximately a month before the passing of Hugo Chávez, Iran sent a special envoy to Havana to meet with President Raul Castro to discuss its next moves in the Americas.[4] Later that year, a spate of visits took place between Tehran and Havana, including a trip by the Cuban vice president to attend the inauguration of Iran's new president, Hassan Rouhani. For his part, Rouhani has not been shy about professing his support for Cuba, issuing a directive in mid-2014 to amend a protocol and increase commercial shipping with the island.[5]

Economic ties likewise are projected to mature. Some six years ago, Iran extended a $768 million credit line to Havana, although the offer was not taken advantage of at the time by the Castro regime. Havana is now seeking to remedy this state of affairs; the Castro regime trying to clear its debt to Iran in an attempt to gain greater economic assistance from the Islamic Republic.[6] This aid will doubtless be provided in exchange for increased Iranian access to the region in a post-Chávez era.

Cuba is currently at the heart of several political developments taking shape in Latin America, with important ramifications for Iran and the region. None, however, are more potentially significant than its attempt to rebrand the flagging Bolivarian alliance by introducing a new construct: the Community of Latin American and Caribbean States, or CELAC. This new regional bloc was born on December 3, 2011, in Caracas, Venezuela, and includes 33 countries from throughout the Americas. In what is an obvious effort to displace the Washington-based Organization of American States (OAS), Cuba's attempts to cement CELAC as the primary forum for political dialogue in Latin America potentially have provided Iran with a new soapbox from which to spread its message, and influence.

Simultaneously, Havana now serves as host for controversial, closed-door negotiations over the future of Colombia. In October of 2012, the government of Colombia initiated talks with that country's half-century-old Communist guerrilla insurgency known as the *Fuerzas Armadas Revolucionarias de Colombia* (FARC). Two years later, these "peace" talks are still ongoing, as the FARC increases its leverage through a recent surge in violence and increased activity in the world of transnational organized crime.[7] Recently re-elected, Colombian President Juan Manuel Santos seems determined to finalize the peace process, a development that would provide Cuba and Venezuela with a proxy force that can also add to Iran's allies in Latin America. Moreover, the FARC's preexisting illicit ties to Iran's proxy Hezbollah mean that "peace" in Colombia would be a net benefit for Tehran as well, providing the Islamic Republic with a new, sympathetic political party in Bogota.

If these political developments run their course, Iran stands to benefit, and the Iranian regime is making preparations to do just that.

A PATTERN OF PENETRATION

Iran's prolonged presence in the region has provided analysts with substantial empirical evidence regarding its preferred pattern of penetration. Much like other extra-regional actors, Iran has exhibited a definitive *modus operandi* in its actions and activities in Latin America.

At the strategic level, this penetration involves a gradual transition from an informal presence to a formal one, while simultaneously focusing on increasing military and paramilitary activities. During the 1980s, Iran initiated this strategy through a covert presence in a handful of Latin American countries under the guise of commercial and cultural exchanges. This cultural penetration allowed Iran, as well as Hezbollah, to embed itself within the Islamic populations of targeted countries. More importantly, it established an infrastructure through which it can insert spies and other subversive actors into the region—operatives who in turn can provide on-the-ground intelligence and in-depth analysis of the challenges and opportunities available to the Islamic Republic in Latin America. This period can be viewed as a collection stage for Iran's presence in the region, one in which Tehran focused on understanding political factors, local populations, indigenous societies, and prevailing socio-economic and demographic trends.

This covert presence was accompanied by an operational component, as witnessed by Hezbollah's successful terrorist attack against the AMIA Jewish center in Buenos Aires, Argentina, in 1994. But the AMIA attack also shed an unwanted spotlight on Tehran's presence, with the effect of significantly slowing the Iranian regime's regional activities thereafter.

At the turn of this century, however, the rise of Hugo Chávez and the ALBA bloc prompted a metamorphosis of Iran's cultural penetration into a more formal diplomatic and economic presence, with the Iranian regime more than doubling its embassies in Latin America and establishing lines of credit with a half-dozen countries in the region. This, however, was coupled with continued covert activity that allowed Iran to establish a command and control structure throughout the region, utilizing both its formal embassies and an informal network of regional mosques and Islamic charities.[8]

Over the last few years, Iran has capitalized on these advancements by also establishing a military industrial footprint in the region. Beginning at least as far back as 2007, Iran signed several joint military-to-military agreements with a handful of nations, most prominently Bolivia and Venezuela. Most of these agreements provided Iran with dual-use materiel for its strategic programs, in exchange for military technology and training given to ALBA nations.[9] For instance, Iran's bilateral military program to help Venezuela develop drone technology resulted in twelve outdated unmanned aerial vehicles (UAVs) called the *Arpia* class. One fourth of these new drones, however, crashed during their first flight tests. Nor are they worth the hefty $28 million the Bolivarian government paid, leaving some analysts to suggest that the joint UAV project provided cover for something else.[10] A mysterious explosion in January 2011 at the site where the drones were being built only served to further fan speculation about the dual-use capacity of the drone factories now operational in Maracay, Venezuela.

Figure 10.1 provides an illustration of how Iran's strategic penetration of Latin America has evolved over time.

At the tactical level, Iran uses its cultural penetration to gain access to prominent individuals within Islamic and indigenous communities throughout the region. The objective is to exploit either wealth or political prominence, preferably both. Once such contact is established, it is used either to bolster Iran's formal diplomatic presence, as is the case in Venezuela, or to establish a new embassy, such as has occurred in Bolivia. Once Iran's formal presence is influential enough to establish financial arrangements, a series of front companies is created. These firms serve as conduits for procurement and acquisition activities, as well as bases for intelligence operatives who insinuate themselves into local societies.[11] Iran's formal commercial presence thereby establishes the plausible deniability necessary to build a military and paramilitary presence robust enough to suit its regional strategic objectives.

At present, Iran has successfully moved through the stages of strategic penetration in the majority of ALBA nations (namely, Cuba, Venezuela, Bolivia, Ecuador, and Nicaragua). In others, the Islamic Republic has had

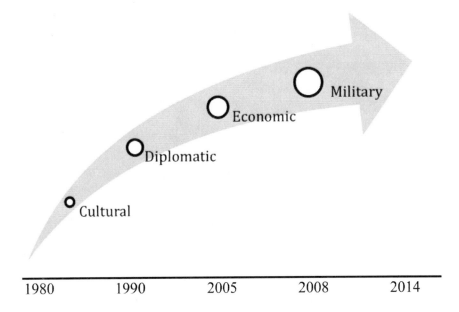

Figure 10.1. **Iran's pattern of penetration in Latin America**

varying levels of success. Nevertheless, it is important to note that the Iranian regime has initiated this process in practically every country in Central and South America.

ESTABLISHING NEW FRONTIERS

Some analysts believed that Chávez's passing would bring about an abrupt end to Tehran's tango with Latin America.[12] More than a year after Chávez's death, however, this has not happened. Rather, Latin America has undergone considerable change—and these political developments can potentially benefit Iran. For example:

- The successful re-election of Ecuadorian strongman Rafael Correa in February 2013 has reaffirmed that Iran can continue to advance its relations with one of Latin America's more successful autocrats through at least 2017. Ecuador's role in challenging the international monetary order also serves to benefit Iran, which has already established several multi-million dollar credit lines with this Andean nation.
- Chile's shift back toward socialist party president Michelle Bachelet in November 2013 potentially allows Iran to gain a stronger foothold in the Southern Cone.[13] As of this writing, only a few months into her new term,

Bachelet has already called for constitutional reform[14]—a tactic often used by Bolivarian countries as a means to consolidate power. There is apprehension, both in Chile and abroad, that Bachelet's second stint as president could turn out to be more radical than her first.

• The June 2014 re-election of Colombia's Juan Manuel Santos also bodes well for Iran, because it represents a reaffirmation of the peace process now underway with the FARC—a process that may end up granting the guerrilla movement enough legitimacy to become a real political force in Colombia. Like Bachelet, Santos has also announced a push towards constitutional reform in Colombia,[15] following in the footsteps of his Bolivarian neighbors. Iran, which already has an embassy in Bogota, will undoubtedly be watching Colombia closely.

The importance to Iran of the recent elections in Ecuador and Colombia was highlighted by a high-level Iranian delegation that traveled to both Quito and Bogota as part of a two week "tour" in mid-2014. This two-nation visit followed a declaration by Alaeddin Boroujerdi, the chairman of the Iranian parliament's National Security and Foreign Policy Commission, that "Iran favors holding a joint meeting of the foreign policy commission of the parliaments of ALBA members in Bolivia."[16]

The Islamic Republic's Iran-Colombia and Iran-Chile parliamentary friendship groups are advancing along a similar track. This is significant, insofar as Chile and Colombia remain the only two South American countries that have not openly opposed the international sanctions levied against Iran for its nuclear activities.[17] They are also core members of the Pacific Alliance, a relatively new political grouping formed in 2011 and envisioned by some as a counterweight to ALBA. Needless to say, better relations between Tehran, Santiago and Bogota would help dilute the potency of this bloc.

Iran's fortunes are brightening elsewhere in the region as well. El Salvador, for example, is a country not typically associated with Iran's presence in Latin America. Yet the narrow electoral victory of President Salvador Sánchez Ceren in March 2014 has solidified the Central American state as a close ally of the ALBA bloc, and by extension drawn it closer to Iran.[18] In the first few months of his presidency, El Salvador has already joined *Petrocaribe* and begun negotiating contracts for increased commerce and cooperation with Venezuela.[19]

Sánchez Ceren's policies are consonant with Iranian objectives. For years, the Islamic Republic has been seeking closer ties to Central America and Mexico for both commercial and strategic reasons. Mexican authorities, however, have consistently rebuffed Iran's advances, including rejecting repeated requests by the regime's ambassador to provide a known proxy, Suhail Assad, a temporary visa to enter the country. In fact, CISEN (the Mexican intelligence service) has placed Assad on a terrorism watch list, prohibiting his future travel to Mexico.[20] As a result, Iran has refocused its attention further south, on El Salvador.

In the past few years, Suhail Assad has visited El Salvador several times in order to establish a local network there, complete with the creation of that country's first Islamic center in the capital, San Salvador. In 2013, Assad was invited by this center to present several lectures at local universities on the "political situation of Iran."[21] It was during this visit that Assad is believed to have begun dialogue with the *Farabundo Marti National Liberation Front* (FMLN), a former Marxist guerilla movement turned political party whose past commander is now president.[22]

Sánchez Ceren's growing alliance with Venezuela, coupled with Iran's soft power strategy in El Salvador, presents yet another opportunity for the Islamic Republic to expand its influence in Central America.

Further south, a similar opportunity is presenting itself in Peru. Peru is typically thought of as friendly to the United States, and its president, Ollanta Humala, has governed in a manner much less radical than was anticipated during his ascension to the presidency.[23] Nevertheless, Peru's close proximity to Bolivia has enabled Iran to quietly establish a growing network of local Muslim converts that travel to Qom to train under the tutelage of Mohsen Rabbani.[24]

Like in El Salvador, Suhail Assad is also deeply involved with the indoctrination and proselytization of these groups. In 2011, Assad began working with indigenous groups within the resource rich Apurimac region of Peru. In September of that year, Assad was the guest of honor at an event organized by the *Casas del ALBA* (a national movement in Peru which expresses solidarity with Chávez's Bolivarian revolution) in Abancay.[25] Edwar Quiroga Vargas, a former socialist activist who converted to Islam, organized the event. Vargas has since made many visits to Iran, leading delegations of as many as 30 Peruvians at a time to Qom and Tehran. Increasing in political popularity, Edwar Quiroga is now positioning himself to run for regional president of Apurimac in October of 2014.[26] Should he win, Iran will potentially gain a local partner in Peru in one of the Andean nation's most resource rich regions.

While the United States continues to be a major trade partner with most countries in Latin America, the dominant narrative in the region is now one of U.S. intervention and espionage; activities that violate the sovereignty of its regional partners.[27] Meanwhile, Iran parrots the rhetoric that "while the U.S. is building a wall with Latin America, Iran is building a bridge."[28]

As the foregoing suggests, this messaging is starting to pay dividends, and the Islamic Republic is quietly gaining ground in Latin America. Even though its primary gateway into the region, the ALBA bloc, is clearly weaker since the death of Chávez in 2013, the sentiments that brought the Bolivarian alliance to power are arguably stronger than ever. Iran is now encountering a new Latin America, one that is increasingly anti-U.S. and anti-Israel in its composition, and one that provides Tehran with numerous opportunities to expand its influence.

PREPARATION OF THE BATTLEFIELD

An old refrain heard in the intelligence community is that "intelligence drives operations," an indication that intelligence operations, by their nature, are meant to provide support to decision makers who plan strategies and particular courses of action. In this context, it is useful to note that Iran's activities in Latin America have historically been focused on intelligence collection and analysis. However, as elsewhere, this preparation is ultimately meant to drive operations in the region. In recent years, therefore, we have begun to see indications of such operations, from the acquisition of strategic minerals to the development of a rapid response capability in the event of a political crisis with either the United States or Israel.

Iran's most likely course of action within the next few years will be to expand its presence in non-ALBA nations, namely Peru, Chile, Colombia, and El Salvador, while keeping its eye on the geopolitical prizes of Argentina, Brazil, and Mexico. At the same time, it seems that Bolivia is quickly becoming Iran's preferred base of operations, giving it further reach into the Southern Cone. Cuba and Venezuela continue to serve as strategic partners of Iran in Latin America, with Ecuador and Nicaragua providing preferential relationships in particular strategic sectors.

Adding up all of these parts, it is clear that Iran is not disengaging from Latin America, but rather reassessing its strategy there to determine how best to advance its interests in the current political and economic climate. Like pieces on a chessboard, Iran is likely to redeploy and reshuffle its assets in Latin America in the years to come. One thing, however, is not likely to change: the fact that the Islamic Republic sees Latin America as a significant strategic arena, and one worthy of sustained attention.

NOTES

1. See Ilan Berman, "Hugo Chávez's Death Is a Blow to Iran," *U.S. News & World Report*, March 12, 2013, http://www.usnews.com/opinion/blogs/world-report/2013/03/12/after-Chávez-a-challenge-for-iran.

2. See Dalga Khatinoglu, "Iran and Venezuela 'Much Ado About Nothing,'" TREND (Baku), May 7, 2014, http://en.trend.az/regions/iran/2271592.html.

3. See Stephen Johnson, *Iran's Influence in the Americas* (Washington, D.C.: Center for Strategic & International Studies, March 2012), 6, http://csis.org/files/publication/120312__Johnson_Iran'sInfluence_web.pdf.

4. "Iranian Envoy Visits Cuba," *Jamaica Observer*, February 19, 2013, http://www.jamaicaobserver.com/news/Iranian-envoy-visits-Cuba.

5. "Rouhani Issues Directives on Iran's Agreements with Burundi, China, Cuba," FARS (Tehran), July 6, 2014, http://english.farsnews.com/newstext.aspx?nn=13930415001233.

6. "Cuba to Repay Debts to Iran: Deputy FM," Tasnim (Tehran), June 28, 2014, http://www.tasnimnews.com/English/Home/Single/415064.

7. Fore more on Colombia's peace process, see Ilan Berman, "Colombia's Perilous Peace," AFPC *Defense Dossier* iss. 9, December 2013, http://www.afpc.org/defense_dossier.

8. This network is detailed in the May 2013 indictment of Argentine prosecutor Alberto Nisman. An English-language translation of the indictment is available online at http://www.defenddemocracy.org/stuff/uploads/documents/summary_%2831_pages%29.pdf.

9. Joseph Humire, "Iranian Weapons on America's Doorstep," *Washington Times*, July 4, 2012, http://www.washingtontimes.com/news/2012/jul/4/iranian-weapons-on-americas-door step/?page=all.

10. Emili Blasco, "Los Drones de Chávez Esconden Algo," ABC.es (Madrid), June 11, 2012, http://abcblogs.abc.es/capital-america/2012/06/11/los-drones-de-Chávez-esconden-algo/.

11. Author's field interviews, Colombia and Brazil, June 2013.

12. See, for example, Ely Karmon, "Chávez and Ahmadinejad: End of a Love Affair," *Ha'aretz* (Tel Aviv), July 3, 2013, http://www.haaretz.com/opinion/Chávez-and-ahmadinejad-end-of-a-love-affair.premium-1.507887.

13. "Iran, Chile Seek Closer Economic Relations," *PressTV* (Tehran), June 16, 2014, http://www.presstv.ir/detail/2014/06/16/367169/iran-chile-keen-to-bolster-ties/.

14. Dan Collyns, "Bachelet Pledges Radical Constitutional Reforms After Winning Chilean Election," *Guardian* (London), December 16, 2013, http://www.theguardian.com/world/2013/dec/16/chile-president-elect-michelle-bachelet-election-reforms.

15. "Colombian President Unveils Constitutional Reform Proposal," FARS (Tehran), June 17, 2014, http://english.farsnews.com/newstext.aspx?nn=13930327000935.

16. "Iranian MPs Leave Tehran for Tour of Latin America," FARS (Tehran), May 26, 2014, http://english.farsnews.com/newstext.aspx?nn=13930305001318.

17. See Tomás Rosa Bueno, "Brazil and Iran: Our Motives and the Bullying Trio," Campaign Against Sanctions and Military Intervention in Iran, June 17, 2010, http://www.campaigniran.org/casmii/index.php?q=node/10378.

18. "Fmr. Marxist Guerrilla Leader to be El Salvador's Next President," *Washington Free Beacon*, February 2, 2014, http://freebeacon.com/national-security/fmr-marxist-guerilla-leader-to-be-el-salvadors-next-president/.

19. "El Salvador y Venezuela Negociaran Acuerdos Sobre Petrocaribe y Commercio," *USA Hispanic*, July 6, 2014, http://usahispanicpress.com/el-salvador-y-venezuela-negociaran-acuerdos-sobre-petrocaribe-y-comercio/#.U7rAJI1dVz6.

20. Wikileaks cable dated March 6, 2009, "Mexico's Relationship with Iran," archived at https://www.wikileaks.org/plusd/cables/09MEXICO674_a.html.

21. "Asociación Cultural Islámica Shiita de El Salvador recibe reconocimiento academico," Revista Cultural Biblioteca Islamica, n.d., http://www.redislam.net/2012/05/notas-culturales.html.

22. Author's interviews with Central American intelligence officials, October 2013.

23. See Roger Noriega, "Peru Heads in Right Direction under Humala," *Miami Herald*, July 24, 2013, http://www.miamiherald.com/2013/07/24/3519315/peru-heads-in-right-direction.html.

24. Author's interviews with former intelligence officials, Lima, Peru, April 2014.

25. See, "Casas de ALBA celebran cita con iraní radical musulmán," *La Razón* (Lima), September 25, 2011.

26. Author's interviews, Lima, Peru, April 2014.

27. For example, see Brazilian President Dilma Rouseff's speech at the 2013 United Nations General Assembly, in which she accused the United States of "meddling" in the affairs of other countries.

28. As quoted by Iran's former Ambassador in Mexico, Mohammad Ghadiri, during an interview with the U.S.-based Spanish-language television station *Univision* as part of its documentary "La Amenaza Irani," released in December 2011.

Chapter Eleven

Crafting a Hemispheric Response

Ilan Berman and Joseph M. Humire

America's response to Iran's intrusion into Latin America is comparatively new. For years, reports of Iran's movements in the region, as well as its growing partnership with regional radicals like Venezuela's Hugo Chávez, garnered only passing attention and interest from officials in Washington. A concerted U.S. policy only emerged in the wake of the September 2011 attempt on the life of Saudi Arabia's ambassador to Washington—an event that awakened policymakers to Iran's growing capabilities south of the U.S. border.

The governmental response took the form of the *Countering Iran in the Western Hemisphere Act of 2012*, introduced in January 2012 by South Carolina congressman Jeff Duncan (R-SC-3).[1] The goal of the bill was to prompt the U.S. government to craft a "comprehensive strategy" to identify, contest, and dilute Iranian activity in Central and South America. The bill passed the House of Representatives easily, and subsequently sailed through the U.S. Senate. It was signed into law by President Obama in December of 2012. The legislation's central provision was the requirement that the U.S. Department of State draft "an assessment of the threats posed to the United States by Iran's growing presence and activity in the Western Hemisphere."[2]

The results, however, were lackluster. The State Department's report, submitted to Congress in June of 2013, depicted Iran's regional presence as being in decline, and downplayed Iran's involvement in fomenting instability in the region.[3] These conclusions contradicted the findings of Argentine state prosecutor Alberto Nisman, whose comprehensive report, released a month earlier, detailed the existence of an extensive and active Iranian terror support infrastructure still active in the region. The findings also ignored evidence that, during the preceding decade, at least three Iranian-sponsored terror plots with links to Latin America had targeted the U.S. homeland.[4]

The resulting Congressional outcry forced Foggy Bottom to backtrack, and commit to a re-evaluation of its findings.[5] As of this writing, however, the Department's revised assessment has yet to be provided to Congress. In the meantime, the damage was already done; in the wake of the State Department's report, momentum toward a real, comprehensive assessment of—and response to—Iran's activities in the Americas stalled noticeably.

So the situation remains. Despite significant Congressional urging, the U.S. government has yet to formulate a comprehensive approach for dealing with Iran's growing footprint in Latin America. It has failed to do so, moreover, despite warnings from the U.S. military and other relevant stakeholders that Iran's influence and interests in the region are more extensive than commonly understood.[6]

But if American policy is stagnant, that of Iran is not. As the preceding pages outline, the Islamic Republic is engaged in a systematic long-term approach to erect and sustain a strategic presence in the Americas. That presence has the potential to hold American foreign policy and national security interests at risk. In its most extreme manifestation, Iran's activities in the region could also pose a direct threat to the safety and security of the U.S. homeland.

The broad, multifaceted challenge posed today by Iran in the Western Hemisphere requires a comprehensive response on the part of the United States capable of addressing the scope and breadth of Iran's contemporary operations and capabilities. Such an approach should focus on a number of priorities.

RE-ENGAGING THE REGION

In the Fall of 2013, in a speech before the Organization of the American States, Secretary of State John Kerry announced with great fanfare that the "era of the Monroe Doctrine is over."[7] Kerry's pronouncement was a distinctly political one, intended to reassure regional powers that the heavy-handed interventionism that at times had characterized America's approach to Latin America was a thing of the past. But it was also very much a sign of the times, because the United States is today in strategic retreat in its own hemisphere.

Since taking office, the Obama administration has systematically disengaged from the Americas, scaling back funding for key initiatives (like the longstanding and highly successful "Plan Colombia"), failing to bolster important partnerships and arrangements, and equivocating over political developments in vulnerable regional states.[8] At the same time, budgetary cutbacks and fiscal austerity have resulted in a significant paring back of the U.S. military's presence and activities throughout the region.

This retraction has not taken place in isolation, as other strategic actors have exploited U.S. disengagement to significantly expand their political and strategic presence in the region. Iran is not alone in this regard; recent years have seen a notable growth in the presence of other extra-regional players in the Americas, such as Russia and China.[9] However, Iran's presence is particularly worrisome given its prominent role in the sponsorship of international terrorism, and the latent synergy that now exists between Iran's radical, uncompromising religious worldview and anti-American leftist elements in the region.

Countering the growth of Iran's influence must begin with sustained attention to the Americas within the Washington Beltway. For too long, the Western Hemisphere has been little more than a foreign policy backwater for the United States. As a result, the United States has tended to ignore or minimize unwelcome hemispheric developments, and consistently has failed to respond quickly and decisively to the growth of regional threats to its vital interests. Re-engagement in the Americas, and reinvestment in its security and prosperity, is therefore a prerequisite for the United States to be able to truly address the problems associated with Iran's presence there.

SUPPORTING A COUNTERNARRATIVE TO ALBA

The strength of the ALBA bloc comes from the ability of its members to establish a narrative that resonates with popular sectors and key demographics within their respective countries.[10] Simply put, ALBA leaders describe themselves as part of an indigenous resistance movement that is liberating the marginalized, oppressed, and impoverished people of the Americas. In their telling, the people of Latin America are illegitimately occupied by regimes that have governed since the Spanish conquest. This narrative provides the ALBA bloc with legitimacy among regional publics, while delegitimizing all prior governments and political alternatives.

The most effective way to counter the ALBA narrative in Latin America is to support a new political alliance that can serve as a counterweight to ALBA's influence in the region. Such a bloc already exists in the recently formed Pacific Alliance, currently made up of Chile, Peru, Colombia, and Mexico (with Costa Rica now in the process of becoming a full member). Born out of frustration with earlier, failed hemispheric trade efforts, the Pacific Alliance is comprised of the region's most open and fastest growing economies. As it currently stands, the countries of the Pacific Alliance have a combined GDP of just under $3 trillion, account for over 50 percent of the region's external trade, and average more than 5 percent annual growth—metrics that far surpass those of ALBA and the rest of the region.[11]

As such, the Pacific Alliance is a logical repository for a robust regional public diplomacy effort aimed at delegitimizing ALBA and its Iranian benefactors. This sort of initiative—carried out via regional media and supported by moderate Central and South American governments—could serve as a potent antidote against Cuba, Venezuela, and other like-minded regimes by promoting stability through social progress and economic freedom.

Regional public diplomacy is, by its very nature, an indigenous enterprise, and one that needs to be carried out by Latin American nations themselves. Where possible and appropriate, however, the United States should encourage and support such messaging, and provide the requisite know-how and funds necessary to erect a truly robust local counter-narrative to "Bolivarian" ideology.

SUPPORTING VULNERABLE REGIONAL ALLIES

The ability of the United States to counter Iran's influence in Latin America will depend in large part on whether it can capitalize on opportunities presented south of the border. The rise of the Pacific Alliance undoubtedly represents one such opportunity. Yet each of the Alliance's members is also currently facing internal problems and conflicts—difficulties that could work against U.S. interests and tilt those countries in Iran's direction.

Colombia, for instance, has experienced a clear downturn in support on security matters from the United States in recent years. Such U.S. assistance, in the form of initiatives such as Plan Colombia, was once a staple in bilateral relations, and largely responsible for the systematic weakening of the Revolutionary Armed Forces of Colombia (FARC) under the presidency of Alvaro Uribe from 2002–2010. Yet such assistance is today in decline, for both political and economic reasons.[12] At the same time, Cuba has taken on an increasingly prominent role, brokering the current peace talks underway between the government of Colombia and the FARC, a process that has provided de-facto legitimacy to the country's half-century-old Communist insurgency. One possible—indeed, likely—outcome of these negotiations is the rehabilitation of the FARC and its incorporation into Colombian politics, a development that would provide a radical movement friendly to Iranian interests and ideals with crucial power and legitimacy.

Similar situations are visible further south as well. In Peru, the Humala government is facing a resurgence of its own guerilla insurgency, the *Sendero Luminoso* or Shining Path.[13] In Chile, a new wave of attacks by armed indigenous groups has brought the government to the negotiating table.[14]

While the United States is largely absent in such regional developments, Iran is not. The Islamic Republic's soft penetration into these countries (either directly or through its proxies) has focused on engaging and aiding these groups. Two particular demographics, women and indigenous groups, are important in this regard. More than half of the population and 60 percent of the electorate in Colombia is made up of women, making this cohort a target not only for politicians but also for the FARC, which has increasingly recruited and deployed females as armed combatants. Indigenous groups hold similar political clout and are intrinsic to current conflicts in both Peru and Chile. These native populations, which serve as an important political base throughout the Andes, are actively being courted by Iran.

A better understanding of these dynamics is vital to any anti-access strategy against Iranian encroachment in Latin America. So is concrete support aimed at stabilizing allied regional governments in the political, security and economic arenas, thereby making them able to better withstand both domestic turmoil and Iran's regional advance.

STRENGTHENED LEGAL FRAMEWORKS

Latin America as a whole is typified by the absence of an overarching approach to terrorism, and much of the region lacks basic legislation criminalizing membership in terrorist groups and providing legal frameworks for their prosecution. A research survey conducted in 2013 by the American Foreign Policy Council found that just eleven of Latin America's twenty-one countries possess laws that make terrorist-related activities a crime under national law.[15]

This has allowed terrorist operatives and assorted radicals to exist in a state of legal grace. Legislatively, acts such as money laundering, narcotrafficking, and counterfeiting, which are often employed by terrorist organizations in fundraising, are generally criminalized. However, no corresponding restrictions or penalties exist for participation in extremist organizations *per se*. (A notable example is the case of Khaled Hussein Ali, a known financier and recruiter for al-Qaeda based in Sao Paulo, Brazil. Despite the publication of an April 2011 exposé in the prominent newsmagazine *Veja* outlining his ties to terror,[16] more than a year later Ali was still residing in Sao Paulo and operating businesses there.[17])

As the foregoing suggests, Brazil remains deeply deficient in the development of a robust legal framework to cover counterterrorism.[18] This is true, moreover, even though a number of legislative proposals have been introduced before the Brazilian parliament in recent years. To date, only six have been reviewed by the Chamber of Deputies, and none have successfully passed into law. Colombia and Mexico similarly lack any sort of anti-terrorism legal framework.

Given the prevailing political realities, however, it is unlikely that the United States will be able to spur a robust counterterrorism policy among

Latin American countries who do not have the political will to engage in that fight. Therefore, a more nuanced approach is necessary—one that links counterterrorism to transnational organized crime. This is because, while terrorism is de-emphasized in many Latin American countries, criminal networks clearly impact most governments in the region and are widely recognized as a top-tier national security priority. By extension, more resources are allocated towards countering transnational organized crime than are to anti-terrorism efforts in Latin America.

For those countries willing to increase counterterrorism cooperation specifically, however, legal assistance from the U.S. government to appropriate agencies and governmental institutions could greatly aid in the establishment and solidification of counterterrorism authorities. The resulting laws would significantly strengthen the legal framework governing counterterrorism in those countries, and provide greater investigatory and prosecution powers to intelligence and security services tasked with addressing the contemporary problem posed by regional terrorism.

RATCHETING UP ECONOMIC PRESSURE

In large measure, Iran's economic intrusion into Latin America has taken place on an informal level, embodied by commercial activities in the region's various free trade zones and numerous gray and black markets. Such activities must be addressed through the imposition of stricter counterterrorism regulations—and the active enforcement of anti-money laundering and counter-threat finance (AML/CTF) rules now in force in other jurisdictions and regions. Also of concern, however, are Iran's formal trade relations with a number of countries in the region—contacts that could provide Iran with access to the U.S. economy and its operatives with greater mobility in the Americas.

A case in point is Ecuador. Ecuador's membership in OPEC, its participation in the ALBA bloc, its dollarized economy, and its lax immigration and visa controls all make it an attractive partner for the Islamic Republic. So, too, does the prominent role that Ecuadorian president Rafael Correa is now seeking to play in the region. For these reasons, the Iranian regime is believed to be carrying out significant illicit financial activities in Ecuador, using banking agreements and bilateral commerce as cover.[19] The United States, however, has the ability to significantly limit Ecuador's interaction with the Islamic Republic. Strong signals from the U.S. Treasury Department about Iran's exploitation of the Ecuadorian economy, and potential consequences for continuing to provide Iran with such access could help to limit bilateral economic relations between Tehran and Quito. This is so because the Ecuadorian public is overwhelmingly supportive of the U.S. dollar, and would represent a powerful constituency against cooperation with Iran if it felt that its standing vis-à-vis the U.S. economy might become threatened as a result. The same holds true for countries like Panama, which has become a hub for much of Iran's money laundering efforts, as well as El Salvador, now actively being explored by the Islamic Republic. Notably, both are also dollarized economies.

APPLYING GREATER SCRUTINY TOWARD FREE TRADE ZONES

Latin America's favorable geopolitical climate, typified by vast ungoverned areas and widespread anti-Americanism, has made it an important focal point of Iran's international activism. So has the region's flourishing informal economy, which affords Iran significant ability to engage in the transshipment and smuggling of contraband. This is especially true in prominent free trade zones throughout the region.

The Paris-based Financial Action Task Force has noted that free trade zones, as currently structured, possess systemic weaknesses that make them vulnerable to abuse and misuse by money-laundering and terrorist financing.[20] The historic "Triple Frontier" of the Southern Cone, Margarita Island off the Caribbean coast of Venezuela, and the emerging tri-border area between southern Peru, western Bolivia, and northern Chile are all prominent free trade zones in Latin America that are exploited by Islamist militants, Hezbollah and Iranian elements among them.

The opportunity for this sort of activity, moreover, is poised to expand significantly. As of this writing, construction is nearing completion on a massive, multi-year expansion of the Panama Canal. Once concluded, it is expected to increase the capacity of the canal from its current volume of four million containers daily to some five times that. According to Panamanian officials, as much as sixty percent of that cargo will be warehoused, at least temporarily, in the nearby free-trade zone of Colon.[21] Notably, there is little indication that Panamanian authorities have a comprehensive strategy to increase screening and customs oversight of the planned expansion of cargo volume.

This state of affairs will provide Iran with an attractive transshipment hub for its strategic programs and contraband commerce, and increases the incentives for Iran to expand its presence in adjacent free trade zones (including Colon). An early indicator of the potential dangers associated with this state of affairs took place in July of 2013, when a North Korean freighter, the *Chong Chon Gang*, was apprehended while transiting through the Panama Canal. The vessel, detained on suspicion of carrying narcotics, was found carrying "sophisticated missile equipment" en route to the DPRK from Cuba.[22]

To prevent future such occurrences, and to ensure that the Canal and other free trade zones are not used by Iran as a proliferation and transshipment point, significant efforts must be made by appropriate U.S. authorities (chief among them the U.S. Department of Homeland Security) to strengthen oversight of port operations and container security, and to provide regional authorities with timely, actionable intelligence on Iranian shipping activities of concern taking place in the Western Hemisphere.

THINKING CREATIVELY

It is a common refrain among members of the U.S. intelligence community that there is no such thing as bad intelligence, only wrong questions. So it has been with the issue of Iran and Latin America. For too long, Iran's regional presence has been measured and quantified based upon metrics such as agreements signed, funds transferred and commerce completed. Lost in this calculus have been the deeper underlying motivations that animate the Islamic Republic's regional presence. These motivations are likely to prove enduring, notwithstanding Iran's potential reconciliation with the West over its nuclear program, or any tactical political shifts that might take place in Tehran.

The events of the past decade have made abundantly clear that the Islamic Republic views Latin America as an important strategic theater, and that it has developed a systematic approach to increase its influence there. Unless and until the U.S. develops a similar strategy of its own, Iran's regional efforts will continue to expand. As they do, so will the threats that they pose to U.S. interests, and to the hemisphere as a whole.

NOTES

1. *Countering Iran in the Western Hemisphere Act of 2012*, H.R. 3783, 112th Congress, Second Session, https://www.govtrack.us/congress/bills/112/hr3783/text.

2. Ibid.

3. Guy Taylor, "State Secrets: Kerry's Department Downplays Iran's Role in Latin America; Likely to Anger Congress," *Washington Times*, June 23, 2013, http://www.washingtontimes.com/news/2013/jun/23/state-department-downplays-iran-role-in-latin-amer/?page=all.

4. The first was the unsuccessful 2007 attempt by an Iranian agent, and Guyanese national Abdul Kadir to blow up fuel tanks at New York's John F. Kennedy Airport. The second was the October 2011 plot by Iran's Revolutionary Guards to assassinate Saudi ambassador Adel al-Jubeir at a DC restaurant. The third was an attempt to hack into U.S. defense and intelligence facilities and launch widespread cyber attacks in the United States in coordination with Cuba and Venezuela, as detailed in a December 2011 investigative documentary by the Spanish-language TV network *Univision*.

5. Josh Rogin, "State Department Ordered Review of Iranian Terror Activity in Latin America," *The Daily Beast*, August 5, 2013, http://www.thedailybeast.com/articles/2013/08/05/state-department-ordered-review-of-iranian-terror-activity-in-latin-america.html.

6. See, for example, SOUTHCOM Commander Gen. John Kelly, posture statement before the House Armed Services Committee, February 26, 2014, http://docs.house.gov/meetings/AS/AS00/20140226/101782/HHRG-113-AS00-Wstate-KellyUSMCJ-20140226.pdf.

7. Keith Johnson, "Kerry Makes It Official: 'Era of Monroe Doctrine Is Over,'" *Wall Street Journal*, November 18, 2013, http://blogs.wsj.com/washwire/2013/11/18/kerry-makes-it-official-era-of-monroe-doctrine-is-over/.

8. See J.D. Gordon, "The Decline of U.S. Influence in Latin America," AFPC *Defense Dossier* iss. 9, December 2013, http://www.afpc.org/files/december2013.pdf.

9. See Ilan Berman, testimony before the House Foreign Affairs Committee Subcommittee on the Western Hemisphere, March 26, 2014, http://docs.house.gov/meetings/FA/FA07/20140325/101958/HHRG-113-FA07-Wstate-BermanI-20140325.pdf.

10. See opening statement of Joseph Humire, testimony before the House Homeland Security Committee Subcommittee on Oversight and Management Efficiency, July 9, 2013, http://www.securefreesociety.org/publications/u-s-house-committee-on-homeland-security-on-irans-extending-influence-in-the-western-hemisphere/.

11. Carlo Dade and Carl Meacham, "The Pacific Alliance: An Example of Lessons Learned," Center for Strategic and International Studies, July 11, 2013, http://csis.org/publication/pacific-alliance-example-lessons-learned.

12. Connor Paige, "Obama Proposes Reducing US Aid Funds to Colombia in 2015," *Colombia Reports* (Bogota), March 4, 2014, http://colombiareports.co/us-president-proposes-reducing-aid-funds-colombia-2015/.

13. Ryan Dube and John Lyons, "'Mutated' Shining Path Resurfaces in Peru," *Wall Street Journal*, May 11, 2012, http://online.wsj.com/news/articles/SB10001424052702304543904577398041485810740.

14. Sam Edwards and Maria del Carmen Corpus, "Bachelet Reveals Indigenous Policy Proposals to Mark Mapuche New Year," *Santiago Times* (Santiago), June 24, 2014, http://santiagotimes.cl/bachelet-reveals-indigenous-policy-proposals-mark-mapuche-new-year/.

15. June 2013 internal study conducted at the direction of Ilan Berman. (Authors' collection.)

16. Leonardo Coutinho, "A Rede o Terror Finca Bases no Brasil," *Veja* (Sao Paulo), April 6, 2011, 89–96.

17. Authors' interview, Sao Paulo, Brazil, April–May 2012.

18. See Joseph Humire, "Antiterrorism in Brazil: A Dangerous Vacuum," AFPC Defense Dossier iss. 9, December 2013, http://www.afpc.org/files/december2013.pdf.

19. See Douglas Farah and Pamela Philips Lum, *Ecuador's Role in Iran's Latin American Financial Structure: A Case Study of the Use of COFIEC Bank* (Washington, D.C.: International Assessment Strategy Center, March 13, 2013), http://www.strategycenter.net/docLib/20130313_EcuadorIran_FarahLam_031213.pdf.

20. See, for example, "Money Laundering Vulnerabilities of Free Trade Zones," Financial Action Task Force *FATF Report*, March 2010, http://www.fatf-gafi.org/media/fatf/documents/reports/ML%20vulnerabilities%20of%20Free%20Trade%20Zones.pdf.

21. Authors' interviews, Panama City, Panama, May 29–30, 2013.

22. Billy Kenber, "North Korean Ship Seized in Panama Canal Carried Suspected Missile-System Components," *Washington Post*, July 16, 2013, http://www.washingtonpost.com/world/national-security/north-korean-ship-seized-in-panama-canal-carried-suspected-missile-system-components/2013/07/16/0234ad22-ee4f-11e2-9008-61e94a7ea20d_story.html.

Index

Agent Banks, 57, 58
Ahmadinejad, Mahmoud, 2, 6, 26, 46, 75, 76; Chávez and, 15–16, 53–54, 63–64
AIC. *See* Anti-Imperialism Center
air strike, Tripoli, 13
ALBA. *See* Bolivarian Alliance for the Americas
alliances: asymmetric networks and, 5; Chávez anti-U.S., 15; El Salvador-Venezuela, 98; FARC- *Foro*, 72; Tehran-Caracas, 15–16, 63–65; U.S. regional, 7, 106–107. *See also* Bolivarian Alliance for the Americas; *specific countries*
Almagro, Luis, 38
American Enterprise Institute, 64, 85
American Foreign Policy Council, 107
Americas: beachhead in, 67–68; building support in, 3–4; motivations for presence in, 1
AMIA. *See Asociación Mutual Israelita Argentina*
AML/CTF. *See* anti-money laundering and counter-threat finance
anti-imperialism, 13, 17, 37
Anti-Imperialism Center (AIC), 13
anti-money laundering and counter-threat finance (AML/CTF), 108
anti-Semitism, 14, 15–17
Argentina, 81–89; CNEA, 78; economy, 82, 83, 84; Islamic extremism

intellectual hub in, 14–15, 36; Israeli Embassy attack in, 14, 41, 81; Rabbani, Mohsen, network in, 36, 40n6, 40n8, 88; Southern Cone strategy and, 35–36, 40n6, 40n8–40n9. *See also Asociación Mutual Israelita Argentina*
Arguello, Jorge, 82
Asociación Mutual Israelita Argentina (AMIA), bombings of, 2, 3, 14, 18, 35–36, 41, 84, 89; controversy over, 86–88; investigations of, 81, 83–84
Assad, Edgardo Ruben "Suhail", 36, 40n6, 40n8, 99
al-Assad, Bashar, 83–84
asymmetric networks, 5
asymmetric warfare, 24, 74–75, 79n3–79n5
At-Tahuid mosque, 36

Bachelet, Michelle, 97–98
Banco Central de Ecuador (BCE), 54–55
Banco Internacional de Desarrollo C.A. Banco Universal (BID), 52–53, 64
Bank Melli Iran ZAO, 55
Barakat, Asad, 37
Basij (people's militia), 29, 75
BCE. *See Banco Central de Ecuador*
BID. *See Banco Internacional de Desarrollo C.A. Banco Universal*
BITCOIN, 60
Bolivar, Simon, 24

113

organized crime and, 29
Thiriart, Jean-Francois, 14
Timerman, Hector, 36, 83, 86, 87
TIPNIS. *See Isiboro Sécure National Park*
Toseyeh Saderat Iran Bank, 52
trade: ALBA economy and, 26, 28–29;
booming illicit, 66–67; with Brazil, 44;
with Chile, 35; free trade zones,
109–110; largest partners in, 34;
NAFTA, 22; Quito-Islamic Republic
agreement for, 56; SUCRE trade model,
57, 58; 2000–2005, 4; U.S.-Latin
American, 99; with Venezuela, 93. *See
also* drug trafficking
Treasury Department, U.S., 25, 43, 52, 54
treaties, 24, 38
Tremlett, Giles, 14
Tri-Border Area (TBA), 27, 34, 39, 44
Triple Frontier, 2, 109
Tripoli, air strike on, 13
Truth Commission, 86
Tudeh Party, 11
Twenty-first Century Socialism. *See*
socialism

UAE. *See* United Arab Emirates
UN. *See* United Nations
UNASUR. *See* Union of South American
Nations
UN Conference on Sustainable
Development, 46
UN General Assembly, 82, 83
UN Human Rights Council, 89
Union of South American Nations
(UNASUR), 58, 72
United Arab Emirates (UAE), 60
United Nations (UN), 16, 44–45, 46, 82,
83, 89
United States (U.S.): anti-U.S. alliances of
Chávez, 15; COMPEBOL funded by,
73; drug investigation in Paraguay by,
37; Latin America reengagement by,
104–105; regional allies of, 7, 106–107;

response to Latin America intrusion, 6,
103–105; SUCRE and, 56, 57, 58;
terrorism plots targeting, 103, 110n4;
trade with Latin America, 99
UN Security Council, 16, 44
uranium ore, 4–5, 38
Uribe, Alvaro, 106
Uruguay, 37–38
U.S. *See* United States

Vahidi, Ahmad, 5, 71, 76, 87
Vargas, Edwar Quiroga, 99
VENEIRAN, 65
Venezuela, 17; Ambassador in Tehran, 30;
asymmetric warfare doctrine of, 74,
79n5; Chávez's government with
Islamic citizens of, 18; El Salvador and,
98; as expansion gateway, 3; immigrant
embarkation point in, 67; Iranian gas
investment by, 26; as military ambition
platform, 63–68; military doctrine of,
24, 74, 79n4; military technology
transport to, 64–65; money laundering
in, 64; nesting scheme failure in, 51,
52–53, 57; partnership with, 4; post-
Chávez era in, 68; Revolutionary
Guards in, 2; shipyards in, 66, 67; trade
with, 93; uranium mining in, 4
VENIRAUTO, 65
Verstrynge, Jorge, 74
virtual currencies, 52, 56–58, 58, 59, 60.
*See also Sistema Único de
Compensación Regional*

warfare, asymmetric, 24, 74–75,
79n3–79n5
Washington, D.C., Borja in, 58
weapons of mass destruction (WMD), 55,
60
Workers' Party, Brazilian, 47

Zambrano, Amenhotep, 30
Los Zetas, 1

About the Editors and Contributors

Ilan Berman is vice president of the American Foreign Policy Council in Washington, D.C. An expert on regional security in the Middle East, Central Asia, and the Russian Federation, he has consulted for both the U.S. Central Intelligence Agency and the U.S. Department of Defense, and provided assistance on foreign policy and national security issues to a range of governmental agencies and congressional offices. Mr. Berman is a member of the Associated Faculty at Missouri State University's Department of Defense and Strategic Studies. He also serves as a columnist for Forbes.com and the *Washington Times*, and as the editor of *The Journal of International Security Affairs*. A noted expert on Iran, he is the author and editor of—among other works—*Tehran Rising: Iran's Challenge to the United States* (Rowman & Littlefield, 2005), *Taking on Tehran: Strategies for Confronting the Islamic Republic* (Rowman & Littlefield, 2007), and *Winning the Long War: Retaking the Offensive Against Radical Islam* (Rowman & Littlefield, 2009).

Leonardo Coutinho is a Brazilian journalist who was responsible for the investigation that exposed the presence of Islamist extremist groups in Brazil. He was also the first to publish official documents that provided evidence of secret visits to Brazil by Iranian cleric Mohsen Rabbani—named by the Argentine Judiciary as one of the architects of the 1994 AMIA attack. Mr. Coutinho has published several articles about corruption, drug trafficking, and transnational crime as a result of detailed investigations in Argentina, Bolivia, Colombia, Paraguay, Panama, and Suriname. He is also the six-time winner of the Journalism Award from *Grupo Abril*, and currently serves as an editor for the Sao Paulo-based magazine *VEJA*.

Joel Hirst is an expert on Latin American policy, having lived in the region for 25 years. Mr. Hirst has been a visiting International Affairs Fellow at the Council on Foreign Relations, where he extensively researched and wrote about Venezuela and the Bolivarian Alliance of the Americas (ALBA). He has also been a visiting Fellow in Human Freedom at the George W. Bush Institute, focusing on Cuba and Venezuela, and served as Cuba team leader and Latin America team member for the 2012 presidential campaign of Gov. Mitt Romney. Mr. Hirst has written extensively on Latin American issues, in both English and Spanish, and appears frequently as an expert analyst on news shows, panel discussions, and other forums in Washington, D.C., and Miami.

Joseph M. Humire is considered one of the foremost experts in the United States on Iran's influence in Latin America. A combat veteran of the United States Marine Corps, Mr. Humire is currently the executive director of the Center for a Secure Free Society (SFS), a Washington based, global think tank. He has conducted a multi-year, multi-pronged investigation on Iran's presence and activities in the Western Hemisphere, and his research on this topic has been sought after by various entities within the U.S. government as well as think tanks, ministries and intelligence agencies throughout the Americas. Mr. Humire has testified on the issue before both the U.S. Congress and Canadian Parliament.

Diego C. Naveira is the coordinator of the parliamentary advisory group for the *Fundación Nuevas Generaciones* in Buenos Aires, Argentina. He is also a lieutenant in the Argentine Army Reserve, and conducts ongoing research on the nexus of security, defense, and the environment. Dr. Naveira received his law degree and doctorate with a specialization in environmental law from the Universidad Católica Argentina (UCA).

Adrián Oliva is a Bolivian lawyer, politician, and human rights activist. Currently a congressman for the Department of Tarija within the national legislature of Bolivia, Mr. Oliva chairs the *Alianza Parlamentaria Democrática de América* (APDA), a regional political platform that defends democracy, human rights, and freedom throughout Latin America. Now a leading opposition member within the Bolivian congress, Mr. Oliva was formerly the deputy minister of internal affairs for the government of Bolivia, and a top advisor for the government of Tarija for several years. Mr. Oliva is the founder of the *Desarrollo Ciudadano Democrático* (DECIDE), an NGO that carries out investigations on human rights, drug trafficking, terrorism, and the role of extra-regional state actors in Bolivia.

Jon B. Perdue is the author of the *War of All the People: The Nexus of Latin American Radicalism and Middle Eastern Terrorism* (Potomac Books, 2012). He is a noted U.S. scholar and researcher on issues of international terrorism, human rights, strategic communication, and peripheral asymmetric warfare. Mr. Perdue serves as the director of Latin America Programs at The Fund for American Studies, and as a senior fellow at the Center for a Secure Free Society in Washington, D.C.

Alex Pérez is the pseudonym for a geopolitical analyst from Ecuador with expertise in security and defense.

Julian M. Obiglio is the president and executive director of the *Fundación Nuevas Generaciones* in Buenos Aires, and was most recently a two-term Argentine congressman from 2007–2013. Native to Argentina, Mr. Obiglio also served on the Parliament of MERCOSUR from 2007–2009 and again from 2012–2013. He holds dual graduate degrees in applied political studies from the *Fundación Internacional y para Iberoamérica de Administración y Politicas Públicas* (FIIAPP) in Madrid, Spain, and business law from the *Escuela Superior de Economia y Administración de Empresas* (ESEADE) in Buenos Aires, Argentina.

Martin Rodil is a Venezuelan counter-threat finance expert with over ten years of cross-functional experience in the governmental, private, and multilateral sectors. His expertise covers Latin American political analysis, research on money laundering operations and terrorism financing, and information gathering from a variety of well-placed sources in Venezuela. Mr. Rodil's research on Iran's activities in Latin America has supported congressional testimony before the U.S. House Homeland Security Committee and the U.S. Senate Committee on Foreign Relations, as well as a series of academic papers. Mr. Rodil has lectured on terrorism, financing, and money laundering before the U.S. Congress, the Center for Security Policy, and the World Affairs Council in Florida, among other venues, and has authored numerous articles on the subject.

Iván Witker is a Chilean political scientist and expert on international terrorism, with a doctorate in social sciences and journalism from Charles University in Prague, Czech Republic. Dr. Witker is currently a professor of international relations at the University of Santiago, as well as a professor and senior researcher at the *Academia Nacional de Estudios Politicos y Estrategicos* (ANEPE) of Chile. He is a graduate of the Center for Hemispheric Defense Studies at the National Defense University in Washington, D.C., and a visiting professor at the Inter-American Defense College.